Presented to:

_____

From:

_____

Date:

_____

POWER PRAYERS

for
Dads

Glenn Hascall

BARBOUR BOOKS
An Imprint of Barbour Publishing, Inc.

ISBN 978-1-68322-864-6

Published by Barbour Books, an imprint of Barbour Publishing, Inc., 1810 Barbour Drive, Uhrichsville, Ohio 44683, www.barbourbooks.com

Our mission is to inspire the world with the life-changing message of the Bible.

Member of the
Evangelical Christian
Publishers Association

Printed in the United States of America.

Contents

Introduction

The Power of a Father's Prayer

You want to be a good dad, to connect with your children, to leave a legacy for them that recalls the *better moments*. In a nod to total honesty you might admit that perfection has eluded you and frustration has replaced good intention. You're here because good dads always look for ways to become better dads. You're looking for tools and this book offers *one* powerful tool with *multiple* applications. The tool? Prayer.

This book encourages conversation. It pays attention to a dad's concerns as well as the high points of God's Word that deal directly with those concerns. You'll meet Bobby, Douglas, Wayne, Jack, Eludi, and Wes. Each of these men bear the likeness of God in the way they responded to His will. Their lives have something to share with dads today.

Men often seem unwilling to ask for directions. This book is a bold declaration that you need to ask God for help—and you can find answers to your questions on fatherhood by asking.

The power prayers offered here are based on scripture. They help bring light to twenty-one different aspects of a dad's life and responsibility. This isn't a five-step plan to parental perfection. It is a practical companion to an improved prayer life—for dads.

Take each aspect as it comes, gain some insight, and then ask God to take it from there. This is a journey. Take the first step. It begins on your right.

My Bible

The Power of God's Road Map

There's a book stolen more often than any other. It's quoted more often, sold more often, and displayed more than any other book. It holds the key to real life, hope for your future, and offers help for each new day.

The Bible was designed to be a road map for the directionally challenged, a go-to resource for discovering who God is, and it contains the exclusive gift God offers to rescue every willing human.

You can read God's Word with a desire to learn—or you *could* leave it unopened while making your best guess. In Isaiah 55:8–9 (MSG) God says, "I don't think the way you think. The way you work isn't the way I work.... For as the sky soars high above earth, so the way I work surpasses the way you work, and the way I think is beyond the way you think."

Guessing about who God is and what He wants will always result in wrong conclusions, wrong actions, and wrong beliefs. God does things differently than you do. It seems strange that the greatest instruction manual you'll ever know has become a common desk ornament instead of wisdom that informs life's decisions.

There are plenty of resources to help you become a better dad. You'll find advice columns, support groups, and a never-ending supply of five-step plans. You'll find quotes, theories, and commonsense guides that celebrate fatherhood. This book was specifically designed to encourage better fathering. However, without God's wisdom, plan, and direction, even this advice will fall short of the mark.

God's plan for dads is unexpected in its generosity. He provides tools, encouragement, and round-the-clock personal assistance. You never have to face new parenting experiences alone. Forget gutting it out, pulling yourself up by your bootstraps, and exploring every shade of self-sufficiency. If you've ever wondered if you could really rely on God for help, Psalm 121:2 (esv) has your answer: "My help comes from the LORD, who made heaven and earth."

The Bible is a treasure hunt without hidden danger. Truth is not out of focus. It's the definitive truth quest for dads. Read it daily for best results. Offer a prayer asking your parenting questions, and begin reading His Word for answers. They're there. They existed even when you weren't looking for them and were unaware you could ask.

In God's Word you'll learn what He expects from you. By learning to pursue Him you'll discover that the rules you follow are the same ones your children need to learn. Your example is as valuable when your children are two as when they're grown and have children of their own. You can be an example because you *have* an example. In Leviticus 19:2 (nlt) God says, "You must be holy because I, the LORD your God, am holy."

Hard? Yes! You're human. Failure is certain. The Bible exists to help you retrace the steps that took you off track so you can rediscover God's true life path. In Matthew 7:14 (niv) the *Creator of dads* says, "Small is the gate and narrow the road that leads to life, and only a few find it."

If the gate is small and the true path leads to life, and if only a few find it, then it isn't much of a stretch to conclude that the Bible is much better read than displayed. Psalm 119:105 (NKJV) says, "Your word is a lamp to my feet and a light to my path." Jesus says in John 14:15 (ESV), "If you love me, you will keep my commandments."

When the Bible is ignored, it can't bring perspective (light) to your decisions. A lack of knowledge will not allow you to show love to the God who made rescue available in the vortex of broken life plans. Many unintentionally walk the wrong path because God's Word remains unread.

Your children need God's instructions as much as you do. Spending time learning together can bring a sense of bonding that few other activities offer. Don't look at God's Word as outdated, irrelevant, or hard to understand. Find a version of the Bible that helps connect you to God's heart. Don't be surprised when it begins to make sense. Don't be surprised when it alters the atmosphere of your home. Don't be surprised when God's idea of a father begins showing up in your bathroom mirror.

The Richest Resource

The revelation of GOD is whole and pulls our lives together. The signposts of GOD are clear and point out the right road. The life-maps of GOD are right, showing the way to joy. The directions of GOD are plain and easy on the eyes. GOD's reputation is twenty-four-carat gold, with a lifetime guarantee. The decisions of GOD are accurate down to the nth degree.
PSALM 19:7–9 MSG

Always Valid

"Heaven and earth will pass away, but my words will not pass away."
LUKE 21:33 ESV

Dear God, You never leave me to sort through expired words, useless ideas, and partial truth. Your wisdom isn't seasonal or generational. You express Your heart in words that mean something to You and can change something in me. The tallest mountain, the fullest ocean, and the most impressive landmarks will all fade from memory before Your words are even a day old compared to eternity. Help me read them with awe and accept them with joy. Amen.

Life Instructions

*Every part of Scripture is God-breathed and useful one
way or another—showing us truth, exposing our rebellion,
correcting our mistakes, training us to live God's way.*
2 TIMOTHY 3:16 MSG

Dear God, there's so much I need to know—and so
much You can teach. Help me learn what to do, what not
to do, and why it's always in my best interest to follow
Your instructions. Your truth is exposed when I read
Your Word. Help me read. Help me understand. Amen.

======

Freedom from the Past

*Get rid of all the filth and evil in your lives,
and humbly accept the word God has planted in
your hearts, for it has the power to save your souls.*
JAMES 1:21 NLT

Dear God, where I have been is not where I want to
return. What I once was is not how I want anyone
to remember me. Help me evict my willingness to break
Your law and accept Your help in transforming the way
I act and speak. May Your ability to rescue bring new
definition to who I will one day be. Amen.

Strength for Today

*"For truly, I say to you, until heaven and earth
pass away, not an iota, not a dot, will pass
from the Law until all is accomplished."*
MATTHEW 5:18 ESV

Dear God, You have given me a purpose, and that purpose
includes today. You want me to make decisions as if there
is still work to accomplish. You write my story, and You
give me the encouragement to live that story. Give me
strength to fully engage with Your plan. Amen.

━━━━━━━━━━

Hope for Tomorrow

*Your word is a lamp to guide my
feet and a light for my path.*
PSALM 119:105 NLT

Dear God, I may not know the destination of where
You're leading, but You've promised to light the path.
My view has limits, but Your willingness to guide never
stops. My hope is anchored in my belief that You care
enough about me to show just what I need to know—
just when I need to know it. Amen.

A Father's Heart

*Blessed be the God and Father of our Lord Jesus
Christ, who has blessed us with every spiritual
blessing in the heavenly places in Christ.*
EPHESIANS 1:3 NKJV

Dear God, Your blessings are a gift I need to recognize.
Some of Your gifts I can see. Some I experience. Some
blessings may not feel like blessings at all. Your Word
is perfect even when it says things I don't like. Your
commands can feel like restrictions. Your ways can
seem confusing. But Your heart expressed in Your
Word confirms that You have always been for me.
That may be one of Your best blessings. Amen.

A Father's Love

*"This is how God loved the world: He gave his
one and only Son, so that everyone who believes
in him will not perish but have eternal life."*
JOHN 3:16 NLT

Dear God, Your Word is crystal clear—You love me. I
might be able to learn this without reading the Bible, but
Your Word makes this truth brighter than the noonday
sun. You ask me to believe in Jesus. You want me to live
in Your presence for all eternity. I don't think I completely
understand Your rescue, but I understand that You loved
me enough to offer what no one else can. Amen.

A Father's Plan

I will instruct you and teach you in the way you should go;
I will counsel you with my loving eye on you.
PSALM 32:8 NIV

Dear God, You have offered to instruct, teach, and counsel
me. You pay attention to my progress. Your plan for me is
greater than my ambition, beyond my ability, and completely
within Your control. The great lessons of obedience can be
found in the Bible. Help me read it for direction. Help me
accept it for purpose. Help me obey it for life. Amen.

═══════════════

A Father's Rescue

For by grace you have been saved through faith.
And this is not your own doing; it is the gift of God,
not a result of works, so that no one may boast.
EPHESIANS 2:8–9 ESV

Dear God, the Bible tells me that You do the rescuing.
Salvation is Your gift to mankind. I can't save myself.
The only thing I can do is trust that You are the Rescuer
and that I can be rescued. And when I want to boast
about the rich life You've given me, help me boast about
the God who made it possible and not the man
who simply accepted Your gift. Amen.

My Salvation

The Power of Authentic Rescue

It is no coincidence that this chapter follows the last prayer. God's rescue is important for you and equally important for your children. His rescue is not merit based, He doesn't grade on a curve, and if you insist on doing life alone, then you'd better be continuously perfect.

The reason you need rescue is that you can *never* be perfect. If you have broken God's law—even once—you're imperfect, and there's no makeup test—no extra credit. First John 1:8–10 (MSG) adds perspective: "If we claim that we're free of sin, we're only fooling ourselves. A claim like that is errant nonsense. On the other hand, if we admit our sins—make a clean breast of them—he won't let us down; he'll be true to himself. He'll forgive our sins and purge us of all wrongdoing. If we claim that we've never sinned, we out-and-out contradict God—make a liar out of him. A claim like that only shows off our ignorance of God."

It actually hurts your children when you fail to make it clear they have broken and will continue to break God's law. Your children should know they need rescue, just like you did, and it's only God's ability to rescue that restores a relationship with Him. It's possible to raise children who are on their best behavior but don't believe they really need rescue. It's also possible to have children who sin but, after breaking God's law, fully recognize they need God's great rescue. The first results in the lifelong self-sufficiency of a lost but decent person. The second results in the forgiveness of one who understands he or she is lost without rescue.

The greatest gift God can offer you is a restored relationship. Over and over again you will discover that the greatest lessons God can teach you are the very lessons you can teach your child. The truths that make a difference in your life will have the ability to impact the lives of those you love.

Everyone sins, and no one can maintain God's benchmark of perfection (see Romans 3:23). The only thing you can earn from sinning is death. God offers a forgiven life through the sacrifice of His Son, Jesus Christ. If you believe that Jesus is God's Son, was sacrificed for your sin, that He rose from the dead, and you trust His ability and willingness to rescue, then you *will* find rescue (see Romans 10:9–10). This is God's rescue plan, and His love for you made it possible.

Romans 10:17 (ESV) says, "So faith comes from hearing, and hearing through the word of Christ." Without hearing or reading about God's greatest gift, you could only develop your own theory about how life works. For instance, if you look at the way you gain an income, you might believe you have to work for your salvation. If you were to look at how you earn a raise, you might think God awards salvation based on the measurement between bad choices and good effort. God is the only One who can offer rescue, and His offer is all-inclusive. The only thing you need to do is accept it. Don't try to reinvent or redefine it.

God's salvation message is ultimately very simple, yet you make it complex when you think you have to *earn* what God is only willing to *give*. Romans 5:8 (NKJV) says, "God demonstrates His own love toward us, in that while we were still sinners, Christ died for us." The verse does not say that God demonstrated His love for you because you did some good things. It doesn't say God demonstrated His love only when you decided to show Him your appreciation. It does say that while you were still in open rebellion to His plan, He loved you enough to send rescue. Why? You would never recognize sacrificial love without Jesus, the Rescuer.

Embrace God's rescue, accept His love, and then use your changed life to tell a story that's not even about you. God's story of rescue is eternity changed for each man, woman, and child who hears, responds, and accepts.

First Corinthians 1:21 (MSG) says, "God in his wisdom took delight in using what the world considered dumb—preaching, of all things!—to bring those who trust him into the way of salvation." What you can do never compares to what Jesus has already done for you.

Wage versus Gift

When people work, their wages are not a gift,
but something they have earned. But people are
counted as righteous, not because of their work,
but because of their faith in God who forgives sinners.
ROMANS 4:4–5 NLT

The Life of the Righteous

He himself bore our sins in his body on the tree,
that we might die to sin and live to righteousness.
By his wounds you have been healed.
1 PETER 2:24 ESV

Dear God, Your Son suffered wounds in both body
and spirit. His death was one of the greatest humilia-
tions of mankind. His example makes it clear that
when I accept authentic rescue, I die to my old life.
My own wounds suffered in the midst of "old life" living
are Yours to heal as You rescue and install an operating
system built on the platform of my new life. Amen.

The Life I Now Live

I have been crucified with Christ and I no longer
live, but Christ lives in me. The life I now live
in the body, I live by faith in the Son of God,
who loved me and gave himself for me.
GALATIANS 2:20 NIV

Dear God, I have stepped in and rescued my children,
sometimes at personal cost. It could have been placing a
hand between them and a nasty fall or telling them no
when it was the best decision I could make. Thanks
for giving me the life I now live. Thank You for giving
Yourself for me and placing Your hands between me
and a death penalty. Thanks for Your wisdom in
sometimes saying no. Amen.

The Need Was Great

If keeping the law could make us right with God,
then there was no need for Christ to die.
GALATIANS 2:21 NLT

Dear God, it honors You when I obey what You've asked
me to do, but I have failed. There are moments when I do
not follow the yield or stop signs You've posted for my
benefit. In those moments, remind me that Your decision
to send rescue through the death, burial, and resurrection
of Jesus was the only answer to my greatest needs—love,
forgiveness, and a restored relationship with You. Amen.

Old Life Living?

*What shall we say then? Shall we continue in sin
that grace may abound? Certainly not! How
shall we who died to sin live any longer in it?*
ROMANS 6:1–2 NKJV

Dear God, help me remember that Your rescue came at a
price. Your free gift was offered because Your Son, Jesus,
sacrificed His life to make it possible. I break Your law
because I'm human. I make poor choices, but help me to
never take Your gift of grace and cheapen it by acting
as if it's a "get out of jail free" card to be used when I
would rather sin than obey You. Amen.

His Measure of Mercy

*He saved us, not because of works done by us
in righteousness, but according to his own mercy.*
TITUS 3:5 ESV

Dear God, You have made it clear my own "gold star"
efforts can never save me. Thanks for infusing mercy into
Your message of salvation. Your rescue is an expression
of Your love and not my effort, Your care and not my
kindness, and Your wisdom and not my knowledge. Amen.

No Other Name

"Jesus is the stone that was rejected by you, the builders, which has become the cornerstone. And there is salvation in no one else, for there is no other name under heaven given among men by which we must be saved."
ACTS 4:11–12 ESV

Dear God, all roads lead somewhere, but only Your road leads to my eternal home. That road is straight, it's narrow, and it bears Your footprints. May I follow them because I completely trust they will lead where no other road can. Amen.

Confess. . .Believe. . .Be Saved

If you openly declare that Jesus is Lord and believe in your heart that God raised him from the dead, you will be saved.
ROMANS 10:9 NLT

Dear God, the best news that has ever happened to me was Your rescue. Help me to never be ashamed to tell others where my new life originates. My belief in Your Son's sacrifice and my trust in Your faithfulness is my acceptance of Your offer to save me. Help me take my gratitude public. Amen.

No Acting

"Knowing the correct password—saying 'Master, Master,' for instance—isn't going to get you anywhere with me. What is required is serious obedience—doing what my Father wills."
MATTHEW 7:21 MSG

Dear God, it is a solemn responsibility to share what I know about You with my children. I want to make Your rescue plan so clear that they can wisely make the choice to accept that plan. I don't want my children to simply act as if they know You. I want them to actually know You. Help me foster an environment in my family that makes it normal for You to find welcome. Amen.

For All

"I want you to know that this salvation from God has also been offered to the Gentiles, and they will accept it."
ACTS 28:28 NLT

Dear God, I am grateful that Your rescue does not discriminate. Any person from any nation speaking any language can believe in You and discover the exact same rescue. The gift was offered to all of us because Your love was for all. Help me represent Your generous gift without discrimination or prejudice. Amen.

My Guide. . .My Hope

Guide me in your truth and teach me, for you are
God my Savior, and my hope is in you all day long.
PSALM 25:5 NIV

Dear God, Yours is a boundless love, enduring grace,
and infinite truth. Mine is a hope that is sure, trust that
believes, and a life that is Yours. While You are perfect, I
am not. So guide me and teach me. You are my God, Your
Son is my Savior, and Your Spirit is my Teacher. I can only
hope, trust, and live by accepting Your love, embracing
Your grace, and following Your truth. Amen.

He Knows Your Voice

I have called upon You, for You will hear me, O God;
incline Your ear to me, and hear my speech.
PSALM 17:6 NKJV

Dear God, there is such a sense of joy knowing that
when I call out to You, You hear me. This is true when
I responded to Your offer of rescue, and it's true every
time I need Your help. My voice is familiar to You. My
concerns are logged into Your record book. My heart
instinctively knows that, when bad times come, I have
every right to call, knowing You hear, understand, and
have instructions for my good and Your glory. Amen.

My Responsibilities

The Power to Engage

Bobby's hair and mustache were devoid of color. From the conversational throne of the barber's chair he listened. He heard the woes associated with farming and a lack of rain. He chuckled at the comments of a trucker. And he got a faraway look when someone brought up his son on a tour of duty overseas.

In time, Bobby mentioned his own time in the army. He had been stationed in Vietnam. He almost seemed embarrassed. Bobby never fought, fired a weapon in combat, or went on any of the missions talked about in history class. He said he "just" administered anesthesia in an army hospital.

Bobby had actually been honored with a Bronze Star for his work during a very difficult and dangerous surgery. As the barber trimmed, Bobby shared bits and pieces of his story: he didn't feel worthy of the medal, he came home early because his wife told him it was either that or she'd leave him (then she left when he came home), he raised three children alone, he never remarried, and he had worked at the city hospital until he retired several years before.

The story Bobby shared was one he hadn't shared often. While he felt he wasn't the hero of the story, his sense of responsibility proved something different.

God placed a high premium on the value of a father to

a child. Bobby faced each day knowing his children would be looking to him to provide food, encouragement, and support. So he did once. So he continued.

In the previous chapter you learned there is no such thing as a perfect person. This truth extends to fatherhood. There is *no* perfect human father. Sometimes they walk away. Sometimes they hurt their children. Sometimes they disengage.

If you're willing, God can take your imperfection and transform your heart so there is a willingness to follow Him. The quality of time you spend with your children may be important, but it can't compare to the quantity of time you can spend. You may not be able to adequately make up for lost time, but you can determine to be there now, and continue to make that decision tomorrow, next week, next month, and next decade.

This is a sensitive subject. Some think fathers are not especially important in the lives of their children. Some like to portray fathers as completely disengaged and the reason their children struggle. While there are arguments that can be made for dismissing a father's value, God makes an argument for your involvement. Proverbs 22:6 (MSG) says, "Point your kids in the right direction—when they're old they won't be lost."

It's your responsibility to give them a moral compass and introduce them to God's GPS. If they aren't introduced, they will struggle to believe God is the direction maker.

There is strength in the blessing of family, and dads gain that benefit. Psalm 127:3–5 (NLT) affirms, "Children are a gift from the LORD; they are a reward from him. Children. . .are like arrows in a warrior's hands. How joyful is the man whose quiver is full of them!" Like arrows, children

27

can be launched in all kinds of world-changing ways, but it starts within family.

Bobby had three children. All of them have grown into responsible adults and have fulfilling careers. What might have happened if Bobby returned from Vietnam and simply walked away from his family? You don't have to guess, because Bobby didn't walk away. Bobby stayed engaged with his children. He sacrificed to make sure they had what they needed to get to the great adult launching pad.

Whatever your family dynamic, God makes it clear that fathers play a crucial role in the lives of their children. You don't have to sit on the sidelines, observe from a distance, or, perhaps worst of all, live disengaged. Your children need you to step up and be their dad.

If all this sounds like hard work, it is. Spend a moment thinking about what is written in Proverbs 23:24 (ESV): "The father of the righteous will greatly rejoice; he who fathers a wise son will be glad in him." You help set a course for your children to follow. Where are they headed?

God Stands with Dads

"Be strong and of good courage; do not be afraid,
nor be dismayed, for the LORD your God
is with you wherever you go."
JOSHUA 1:9 NKJV

Dear God, You give me permission to be courageous. You
tell me fear is unnecessary. You tell me there's no need to
panic. You are with me—wherever I go. In those moments
when I am weak, help me remember that Your strength
offers courage, trust, and confidence. Thanks for Your
companionship. I have always needed it. Amen.

Family Declaration

"As for me and my house, we will serve the LORD."
JOSHUA 24:15 ESV

Dear God, help me declare my intent to follow You
so my children know for certain that I have chosen
a side. May they see that my love for You means I
accept Your help and choose to follow Your way. May
they be encouraged by a proclamation that I want my
family to be known as followers of Jesus Christ. May I
find ways for my family to work together to serve
You and the people You love. Amen.

Give It All You've Got

*Keep your eyes open, hold tight to your convictions, give it
all you've got, be resolute, and love without stopping.*
1 CORINTHIANS 16:13–14 MSG

Dear God, help me see what I need to see, believe what
I need to believe, give what I need to give, and love as
long as I live. May this be more than my responsibility
as one who follows You, and may it serve as the right
example for my children. May they see that I am engaged
in a friendship with You and that I am engaged
in my relationship with them. Amen.

Delight to My Soul

*The LORD corrects those he loves, just as a
father corrects a child in whom he delights.*
PROVERBS 3:12 NLT

Dear God, I love my children. I want to see them succeed.
Help me remember that the way I fulfill my role as a
father is patterned after You. You don't always give me
what I want, but what You offer is always better. Help me
say no when I need to and yes when possible to the children You've given. They bring delight to my soul. Amen.

The Greatest of Fathers

"Which one of you, if his son asks him for bread, will give him a stone? Or if he asks for a fish, will give him a serpent? If you then, who are evil, know how to give good gifts to your children, how much more will your Father who is in heaven give good things to those who ask him!"
MATTHEW 7:9–11 ESV

Dear God, I don't want to be amused at the discomfort my children might feel if I deny the most simple request. Help me understand that You care about the small stuff. You want me to ask You for help and then acknowledge the place where rescue came from. Thanks for helping me understand that the way I feel about my children is not unknown to the greatest of fathers. Amen.

The Compassionate Heart

As a father has compassion on his children,
so the LORD has compassion on those who fear him.
PSALM 103:13 NIV

Dear God, I am grateful for Your compassion. Help me take what I've learned from You and show that same compassion to those You've allowed to call me "Dad." Thank You, Father. Amen.

More Than I Do

"Look at the birds of the air, for they neither sow nor reap nor gather into barns; yet your heavenly Father feeds them. Are you not of more value than they?"
MATTHEW 6:26 NKJV

Dear God, can I just admit that being a father is hard? I always wonder if I'm doing it right, and when I make mistakes I feel like a failure. It can make me want to give up, but don't let me. You have promised to take care of me and my family. You promise to guide me. Help me learn from my mistakes and remember who cares about my family more than I do. Amen.

Serious about the Follow

Don't love the world's ways. Don't love the world's goods. Love of the world squeezes out love for the Father.
1 JOHN 2:15 MSG

Dear God, there are ways of dealing with issues that please You and ways that don't resemble Your action plan at all. Because my children watch to see what I do, help me keep in mind that the things I do, the stuff I like, the places I go will either show them I'm serious about following You, or that I don't believe it's that important. For their sake, and for my good, help me be responsible with my choices and own up to my mistakes. Amen.

Where I Am Now

*What you have learned and received and
heard and seen in me—practice these things,
and the God of peace will be with you.*
PHILIPPIANS 4:9 ESV

Dear God, help me find other men who have followed
You longer than I have. Help me learn from them, and
may their wisdom encourage me to be the kind of father
You always meant for me to be. Because I'm responsible
for following You, and for being an example to my
children, prompt me to be proactive in learning what I
can from men who've been where I am now. Amen.

The Blessing of Being Selfless

*"Let your light shine before others, that they may see
your good deeds and glorify your Father in heaven."*
MATTHEW 5:16 NIV

Dear God, I want my children to see the blessing
of being selfless. Help me share with others so my
children may come to see this act as normal and
worth following. May they understand that being
selfless or humble is not about creating a show but
about sharing gifts that You gave first. Amen.

My Marriage

The Power of Unity

Love isn't a puppy, cute to look at with no real understanding that puppies are born with bad behaviors they don't want you to notice. Love isn't a flower, beautiful today but faded and lifeless too soon. Love isn't blind but sees clearly and forgives quickly.

It's been said that marriage is the connection between two good forgivers. Love is a choice that may trigger beneficial feelings, but it's never guaranteed. God inspired John to write in 1 John 3:18 (NIV), "Let us not love with words or speech but with actions and in truth."

Don't be confused by what you feel. Love chooses to be kind when you feel like turning your back and chilling your shoulder. Love gives when it would be easier to withhold. Love doesn't post a list of conditions.

You can alter the future for your children by making the daily choice to love your wife. It helps children learn the art of selflessness. When your children see you sacrifice your interests on behalf of your family, it opens a more accurate view of love to the heart of a child. The return on this investment can extend to multiple generations.

Love is less romantic gesture and more elbow grease. When you compare and contrast the love statements of 1 Corinthians 13 it might look like this:

When you're in a hurry, love is patient. When you're frustrated, love is kind. When you're envious, love chooses contentment. When you want to list your accomplishments, love changes the subject. When you sense pride in your life, love chooses humility. When you want to dishonor others, love chooses to acknowledge their gifts. When you want your own way, love chooses to listen to the needs of others. When you want to give in to anger, love walks the path of peace. When you want to keep a spreadsheet listing the offenses of others, love chooses the delete key. When you think it might be fun to see bad things happen to someone, love rejoices in God's forgiveness. When you want to step aside and let someone get hurt, love protects. When you want to build walls to keep people out, love chooses to trust God with the outcome. When you want to give up, love embraces hope. When life gets tough, love perseveres.

Prayer is essential to loving others. Why? True love does not come naturally to humans. You can be attracted to, have good feelings about, and even enjoy the company of someone else, but those experiences don't come close to God's description of love. Praying and asking God for His help will be important in order to move you from *love as you know it* to the love God has in mind.

Jesus says in Matthew 22:37–39 (MSG), "'Love the Lord your God with all your passion and prayer and intelligence.' This is the most important, the first on any list. But there is a second to set alongside it: 'Love others as well as you love yourself.'"

There are three words here worth a closer look—*passion*, *prayer*, and *intelligence*. It seems that emotion, spiritual conviction, and a choice of the mind are included in a decision to obey God by loving Him and His people.

By the way, the Matthew 22 passage was in response to a question: "What is the greatest command?" Love isn't just a good answer, it isn't something you hope for, and it's not something you make people earn. Love is God's greatest command for His people. It changes the heart of those you choose to love. It will change you.

Don't think of your marriage in terms of a romance novel, movie, or something that compares favorably to your idea of perfection. If you do, you can expect disappointment. Your kids can bear with the flaws you expose in accepting God's command to love your wife. The unity found in a marriage that chooses *love* instead of *feelings* can be the greatest object lesson about God's love you could ever experience. He stands with the faithless, loves the unloving, and made the choice to restore love before the earth was ever created (see Ephesians 1:4).

Because love is more than words, because a glance across the room only proves you can see, and because your children pay careful attention to what you do—love deeply, be compassionate, and bear with the faults of those God calls you to love (see Colossians 3:12–14).

The Great Example

I am convinced that nothing can ever separate us from God's love. Neither death nor life, neither angels nor demons, neither our fears for today nor our worries about tomorrow—not even the powers of hell can separate us from God's love. No power in the sky above or in the earth below—indeed, nothing in all creation will ever be able to separate us from the love of God that is revealed in Christ Jesus our Lord.
ROMANS 8:38–39 NLT

What You Want Me to Do

Beloved, let us love one another, for love is from God, and whoever loves has been born of God and knows God.
1 JOHN 4:7 ESV

Dear God, help me remember that love is Your big idea. It is easy to resist, speak unkindly, or even hate others. It's much harder to make the choice to love even when I know it's what You want me to do. You made the rules for love and said it's something I must choose to do—in Your name. Amen.

The Genuine Choice

Let love be genuine.
ROMANS 12:9 ESV

Dear God, You don't want me to "fake it till I make it."
You want me to choose love as something I do, not
something I feel. Love is most genuine when it's a choice.
Love can lack authenticity when I insist on thinking I
must feel something that seems like love in order to be
kind. Help me love my wife so my children can see they
always have an authentic choice to do the same. Amen.

Prevent Me from Withholding Love

*"This is how everyone will recognize that you are my
disciples—when they see the love you have for each other."*
JOHN 13:35 MSG

Dear God, prevent me from withholding love from
those I encounter. May this be especially true of my
own family. It can be easy to think someone needs to
earn my affection. I want to be identified as a man
who follows You. Let me follow You to the place of
unconditional love, in my family first and then
beyond the walls of my home. Amen.

Honor as Normal

Outdo one another in showing honor.
ROMANS 12:10 ESV

Dear God, help me show honor to my wife. May I abort any mission whose goal is to find and expose her faults. I want to learn how to lift her up and care for her so that she recognizes the honor. I want my children to see honor as a normal part of Your love plan. Amen.

———————————

Heavy on Encouragement

Each man must love his wife as he loves himself.
EPHESIANS 5:33 NLT

Dear God, I don't want to hurt the ones I say I love. If I am to love my wife in the same way I ensure my own needs are taken care of, I can only imagine how different things could be. To nurture her dreams, inspire her voice, and pay attention to her heart would go a long way in improving her willingness to communicate with me. Help me offer a relationship heavy on encouragement. Amen.

What Forgiveness Looks Like

*Be gentle with one another, sensitive. Forgive one another
as quickly and thoroughly as God in Christ forgave you.*
EPHESIANS 4:32 MSG

Dear God, remind me—in those moments I choose
to keep forgiveness from my wife—that You have
never denied me the gift of forgiveness. Help me not
keep lists of wrong, hold grudges with stubborn pride,
and believe I am a victim. Like all Your best gifts,
You showed me what forgiveness looks like so I can
recognize when I need to offer it. Amen.

Most at Peace

"Do to others as you would like them to do to you."
LUKE 6:31 NLT

Dear God, my child has witnessed times when I made the
choice to withhold love. I regret the missed opportunity
to show that treating others with respect was Your idea.
Help me learn this truth, share this truth, but most im-
portantly live this truth. I am most at peace in my
marriage when my wife is sure I am on her side. Amen.

Loyal Love

Don't lose your grip on Love and Loyalty. Tie them
around your neck; carve their initials on your heart.
PROVERBS 3:3 MSG

Dear God, loyalty is a choice. So is love. Let me
remember that loyalty is a tangible aspect of love.
Let me wear loyal love around my family. May they
never have to question my commitment to them. I will
fail, so let me be grateful that Your loyal love is mine, and
then let me share that loyal love with my family. Amen.

Love Has Always Existed

Love never ends.
1 CORINTHIANS 13:8 ESV

Dear God, You are the best description of love.
You have always existed, and You always will exist.
Because you are love, it only makes sense that love
will never end. You loved me before I was ever born.
You loved me when I didn't know You. You loved me
when I broke Your law. Since love never ends, help
me believe it, accept it, and share it. Amen.

Undeserved—Highly Valued

Serve one another humbly in love.
GALATIANS 5:13 NIV

Dear God, I'm beginning to get the idea that You
want me to love. I'm beginning to think that it's
important to You because it's a gift that is undeserved,
yet highly valued. I believe love is a service that
is offered without qualification. Help me love
others and give the credit to You. Amen.

Love and Be Loved

We, though, are going to love—love and be loved.
First we were loved, now we love. He loved us first.
1 JOHN 4:19 MSG

Dear God, You want me to give love and You want me
to receive love. I'm convinced that—since You loved me
without any assurance I would love You back—I can make
the choice to love my own family. With Your help, "love"
and "being loved" can be permanent houseguests. Amen.

My Children

The Power of Modeling

The picture of a child standing in the shoes of his father is a powerful image. It has its own sense of *cute*, but it also indicates this child will grow to adulthood and bear both the likeness and the mannerisms of the man who owned the shoes he sought to fill.

You follow God because you want to be like Him. Your children follow your example because they want to be like you. In the end, your desire should be that your children move beyond imitating you to following God.

The Bible places great emphasis on a father's need to model what a relationship between God and mankind looks like. Make learning and following God's plan a priority. Make modeling a logical next step to what you learn. Don't think perfection is the only way you will ever be able to model Christlike character. Deuteronomy 6:6–8 (MSG) says, "Write these commandments that I've given you today on your hearts. Get them inside of you and then get them inside your children. Talk about them wherever you are, sitting at home or walking in the street; talk about them from the time you get up in the morning to when you fall into bed at night."

These instructions say that you should get God's Word into yourself first and then your children. God's instructions aren't just for a weekend church service. Instead, they exist for daily instructions and they exist for modeling the spiritual growth you want for your family.

Perhaps the most practical reason for getting God's Word from the pages of your Bible into your heart and ready for sharing is found in Psalm 119:11 (ESV): "I have stored up your word in my heart, that I might not sin against you."

If God's Word is good for you, imagine how life changing it will be for your children. What you read, remember. What you discover, share. What your God says, obey. The Bible stories you read can be great object lessons, but you don't have to stop there. And if more is caught by what children see than taught by the words you speak, then modeling is a perfect dad thing to do.

You wouldn't ask your children to go to the workshop and return with a handcrafted doghouse if you hadn't taught them how to safely use the tools needed to finish the project. This would be dangerous and unproductive. God didn't insist you live the Christian life without instructions. A dad's job is to model, teach, and work through mistakes along the way. Sometimes you'll learn more than your child just by being willing to model God's character.

In Ephesians 5:1–2 (NLT) the apostle Paul wrote, "Imitate God, therefore, in everything you do, because you are his dear children. Live a life filled with love, following the example of Christ. He loved us and offered himself as a sacrifice for us."

When you do what God does, you are following a loving example, just like a child imitates his own father. The way you model God's example should be infused with love and a willingness to do what's best for your family.

Your children will look to you as the best example of

what it looks like to be a grown-up. What you do and how you do it will leave an impression on young minds and impressionable hearts. You can't change that. What you can change is the example they see, and that change in example will leave you with no regrets.

Galatians 2:20 (NKJV) says, "I have been crucified with Christ; it is no longer I who live, but Christ lives in me; and the life which I now live in the flesh I live by faith in the Son of God, who loved me and gave Himself for me."

Becoming a model of Christlike character means your life perspective has been radically altered in an *eternity-changing encounter* with God's Son, Jesus. You still have a sinful nature, but that nature has been tempered by a new trust in the One who loved you and willingly sacrificed Himself so that you could learn to be the example your children need.

Make no mistake, you *will* be an example for your children. You could choose your best effort—or God's perfect model.

Building on Basic Faith

Don't lose a minute in building on what you've been given,
complementing your basic faith with good character, spiritual
understanding, alert discipline, passionate patience, reverent
wonder, warm friendliness, and generous love, each dimension
fitting into and developing the others. With these qualities
active and growing in your lives, no grass will grow under
your feet, no day will pass without its reward as you mature
in your experience of our Master Jesus. Without these qualities
you can't see what's right before you, oblivious that your
old sinful life has been wiped off the books.
2 PETER 1:5–9 MSG

Fully Developed

Oh, my dear children! I feel as if I'm going through
labor pains for you again, and they will continue
until Christ is fully developed in your lives.
GALATIANS 4:19 NLT

Dear God, instill in me a passion for making You
welcome in my home. May I cooperate with You to
make it a natural part of home life to include You.
May my actions reflect Your character and my words
acknowledge Your help. I ask because I want to see
Jesus fully developed in the life of my child and I
never want to be a stumbling block. Amen.

Living "Different"

*Those who say they live in God
should live their lives as Jesus did.*
1 JOHN 2:6 NLT

Dear God, remind me that when I respond the way
You respond, and live the way Your Son showed me
to live, I am being transformed because I am obeying
You, but I am also representing the value of Your
rescue plan to my own family. Amen.

Don't Go It Alone

"Take my yoke upon you and learn from me."
MATTHEW 11:29 NIV

Dear God, thanks for reminding me that I can learn
from You. Thanks for making it clear that Your Son
will walk with me as a teacher, leader, and guide. There
are so many times I think I have to figure things out
on my own and then hope I'm teaching my family the
right things. I am grateful I don't have to guess
and that I don't have to walk alone. Amen.

The Faith Plan

*He creates each of us by Christ Jesus to join him
in the work he does, the good work he has gotten
ready for us to do, work we had better be doing.*
EPHESIANS 2:10 MSG

Dear God, since You have a plan for my life, it's easy to
understand You also have a plan for my children. You
are welcome to use me to introduce some of that plan
to them. Help me join You in Your work and invite
my kids to help in ways only they can. Amen.

Keep Working, God

*I am sure of this, that he who began a good work in
you will bring it to completion at the day of Jesus Christ.*
PHILIPPIANS 1:6 ESV

Dear God, You have the self-imposed assignment
of making me a new creation. Once You start,
You keep working until one day I will be a finished
design with You in heaven. May I successfully teach
my children that they need to be made new too.
Cooperating with You is the best thing I can do
to change the hearts of my children. Amen.

God's Spiritual Classroom

For God is working in you, giving you the
desire and the power to do what pleases him.
PHILIPPIANS 2:13 NLT

Dear God, the more time I spend in Your classroom,
the more I find I want to do what pleases You. I
want to keep inviting my children to join me in these
moments of instruction. One of my greatest desires is
to see them enthusiastically learn from You. Amen.

Represent

"He must become greater;
I must become less."
JOHN 3:30 NIV

Dear God, I expect my children to look to me for
guidance, but I want to keep moving them from
dependence on me to dependence on You. Help me step
back as You become more real to my children. May I
always remember I represent You to my children. Amen.

Like My Teacher

*"A disciple is not above his teacher, but everyone
who is perfectly trained will be like his teacher."*
LUKE 6:40 NKJV

Dear God, I always want You to be my model for a
quality Christian life. I can never be greater than You,
but as You train me I can become more like You.
May my children become disciples of You and may
I be a willing disciple in training. Amen.

He Didn't Claim His Rights

*He didn't claim special privileges.
Instead, he lived a selfless, obedient life.*
PHILIPPIANS 2:7 MSG

Dear God, when Your Son, Jesus, came to earth He
could have been very intentional about letting people
know who He was and that they needed to honor Him,
but He didn't. He came without claiming His rights.
He came to model a selfless and obedient life. You must
have known dads would need this example. Amen.

My Home

The Power of a Spiritual Atmosphere

You've heard that your home is a castle. That's a pretty good word picture for the way God designed your home to function. A castle has a moat, drawbridge, gates, and guards. If you're wondering what these castle elements have in common, it has everything to do with effectively keeping the enemy away from those who take refuge within the walls. Your castle should be a safe place for those who call the inside home.

Dads can do this only by keeping in close contact with God. The psalmist used his own word canvas to describe this connection: "God is our refuge and strength, an ever-present help in trouble. Therefore we will not fear, though the earth give way and the mountains fall into the heart of the sea" (Psalm 46:1–2 NIV).

If you're like most dads, you want to protect your children. The last thing you would ever want is for harm to come to your family. Maybe that's why you are in charge of your personal castle. You might purchase a security system. You might check the doors and windows before you go to bed. You don't let just anyone come into your home.

However, there are a few areas where guardians might slip in their dedication to protection. One example includes mobile phones, video games, computers, and television. Each contain windows where the enemy can invade your home without your objection. Sometimes without your knowledge.

Philippians 4:8 (ESV) provides God's design for the protection of your family: "Finally, brothers, whatever is true, whatever is honorable, whatever is just, whatever is pure, whatever is lovely, whatever is commendable, if there is any excellence, if there is anything worthy of praise, think about these things."

It's possible this sounds prudish and overprotective, but if you're serious about providing a spiritual atmosphere that honors God, then what you allow in your home deserves as much consideration as a security system.

Some things are overlooked by dads. It may be because what has been overlooked is where personal compromise exists. If you were to reset the direction of what your children see, play, visit, and talk to, it would also mean that you would have to personally reset in the same areas. Why? If there are two sets of rules in the family, you weaken your role as a model for your children to follow.

Children expect you to play by the same rules they are told to follow. They can and will spot hypocrisy. When they do, you can expect them to bring it to your attention and choose to follow your actions over your words.

How serious does God take the issue of spiritual health? Ephesians 6:10–12 (MSG) says, "God is strong, and he wants you strong. So take everything the Master has set out for you, well-made weapons of the best materials. And put them to use so you will be able to stand up to everything the Devil throws your way. This is no afternoon athletic contest that we'll walk away from and forget about in a couple of hours."

Your adversary is real, but God has given you all the

weapons you need to defend your family: "Put on every piece of God's armor so you will be able to resist the enemy in the time of evil. Then after the battle you will still be standing firm. Stand your ground, putting on the belt of truth and the body armor of God's righteousness. For shoes, put on the peace that comes from the Good News so that you will be fully prepared. In addition to all of these, hold up the shield of faith to stop the fiery arrows of the devil. Put on salvation as your helmet, and take the sword of the Spirit, which is the word of God" (Ephesians 6:13–17 NLT).

What's good for children is good for Dad. As difficult as it may be to protect every area of family life, your children will gain more benefit from your God-directed obedience than compromise that leaves them open to attack.

There is one more bit of spiritual advice from Ephesians 6, in verse 18 (NIV): "Pray in the Spirit on all occasions with all kinds of prayers and requests." (For yourself, for your wife, and for your children—pray and invite God's involvement.)

Be Strengthened

*For this reason I bow my knees to the Father of our Lord
Jesus Christ, from whom the whole family in heaven and
earth is named, that He would grant you, according to the
riches of His glory, to be strengthened with might through
His Spirit in the inner man, that Christ may dwell in
your hearts through faith; that you, being rooted and
grounded in love, may be able to comprehend with all
the saints what is the width and length and depth and
height—to know the love of Christ which passes knowledge;
that you may be filled with all the fullness of God.*
EPHESIANS 3:14–19 NKJV

Wisdom to Protect

*By wisdom a house is built, and by understanding
it is established; by knowledge the rooms are
filled with all precious and pleasant riches.*
PROVERBS 24:3–4 ESV

Dear God, I want my house to be a home. I want to
protect those gathered under its roof. I want the wisdom
to know how to lead, the understanding to establish
protection, and the knowledge that the family members
You have given me are precious. Help me pay attention to
those things that seek to lure us away from You. Amen.

The Guardian

Be on your guard; stand firm in
the faith; be courageous; be strong.
1 Corinthians 16:13 niv

Dear God, in order for me to fail in my role as protector,
I would need to be overtaken. My guard would need to
be down. My responsibility overlooked. In my family and
for my children, help me be courageous, strong, and a
guardian for each member of my family. Amen.

Awe Inspiring

How joyful are those who fear the Lord and delight in
obeying his commands. Their children will be successful every-
where; an entire generation of godly people will be blessed.
Psalm 112:1–2 nlt

Dear God, it's good to know that others have
struggled with being human and still found You to
be an awe-inspiring and worthy leader. Thanks for
reminding me that my choices today impact my
children and the people they influence. Amen.

Faithful Guardian

The Lord is faithful. He will establish
you and guard you against the evil one.
2 Thessalonians 3:3 esv

Dear God, as alert as I may be, help me remember
that ultimately You are my family's greatest protector
and guardian. My actions will always serve as a model,
so I want to follow You closely, but I can never protect
as well as You. I can never guard against evil as well
as You. Help me stand firm as I watch You
faithfully guard my family. Amen.

―――――――――――――――

When Feelings Lie

"Be strong and of good courage. . . .
[God] will not leave you nor forsake you."
Deuteronomy 31:6 nkjv

Dear God, on those days when I feel alone, help me
remember my feelings can lie to me. No matter how
I feel, help me stand strong. May I find the courage I
need because You have promised that You're not going
anywhere. Help me demonstrate to my children
that You can be trusted. Amen.

On Loan

Fathers, do not provoke your children to anger by the way
you treat them. Rather, bring them up with the discipline
and instruction that comes from the Lord.
Ephesians 6:4 nlt

Dear God, thank You for reminding me that being
a protector for my family doesn't mean I should make
my children miserable. Remind me that reflecting
Your love to my children is better than ruling in a
way that inspires fear, reduces trust, and encourages
rebellion. My children are on loan to me from You.
Help me lead them—to You. Amen.

Avoiding Stupid

Exploit or abuse your family, and end up with a fistful of air;
common sense tells you it's a stupid way to live.
Proverbs 11:29 msg

Dear God, if my home is a castle where I protect my
family, then help me learn enough from You to protect
them from the worst possible me. I am a human charged
with protecting humans. Help me study Your Word
enough to know that taking advantage of my
family is always a bad idea. Amen.

The Dad I Need to Be

I can do all things through Christ who strengthens me.
PHILIPPIANS 4:13 NKJV

Dear God, when I feel like being a dad is just too much,
when I feel like I can't go on, when I want to give up, I
need You to remind me that You are my strength and the
One that helps me be the kind of dad I need to be. Amen.

When They See You in Me

The father of the righteous will greatly rejoice;
he who fathers a wise son will be glad in him.
PROVERBS 23:24 ESV

Dear God, I know that having children is no guarantee
they will follow You, but when I choose to make You a
priority, there are so many more reasons to rejoice when
they see You in me. When they choose what's right over
what's easy and when they accept wisdom instead of
daily trends, I will rejoice. I will be glad. Amen.

Love Evicts Fear

There is no fear in love. But perfect love drives out fear,
because fear has to do with punishment. The one who fears is
not made perfect in love. We love because he first loved us.
1 John 4:18–19 niv

Dear God, my children need to experience a father's
love. You tell me in Your Word that the greater the
love, the further fear moves away. Where loves reigns,
fear must leave. When fear withholds trust, please give
love permission to tear down walls and build bridges.
Where fear crushes a spirit, help love heal the wounds.
Help me love my family in such a way that fear
seeks an exit from our home. Amen.

Words Are Cheap

Let's not merely say that we love each other;
let us show the truth by our actions.
1 John 3:18 nlt

Dear God, I know that words are cheap. I have been
guilty of making promises I haven't kept. There are times
my mouth says one thing and my actions speak another
language. May the words I speak and the things I think
lead me to actions that confirm in the minds of my
children that I love them and I'm not just saying words
they want to hear. I will need Your help. Amen.

My Availability

The Power of Time

If you're a dad struggling to find enough time to spend with your wife, finish work, enjoy hobbies, learn from God, appreciate friendships, eat, sleep, and take a shower, then you're in good company. Wait, what about the kiddos?

This is where the struggle becomes visual, tangible, and typical. To compensate, a lot of dads will substitute *time* with *stuff*. It can be misleading when a child receives a gift from Dad and seem overwhelmingly happy. Dads are left believing they have just hit a home run and that the gift erased the disappointment associated with previous broken promises.

Instinctively you know that children want to spend time with you, but you've paid too much attention to life hacks—hacks suggesting you can have it all if you just find the right series of tricks to make life work.

Ecclesiastes 3:1–8 (MSG) says, "There's an opportune time to do things, a right time for everything on the earth: a right time for birth and another for death, a right time to plant and another to reap, a right time to kill and another to heal, a right time to destroy and another to construct, a right time to cry and another to laugh, a right time to lament and another to cheer, a right time to make love and another to abstain, a right time to embrace and another to part, a right time to search and another to count your losses, a right time to hold on and another to let go, a right time to rip out and another to mend, a right time to shut up and another to speak up, a right time to love and another to hate, a right time to wage war and another to make peace."

Let your mind make the needed connections between where you are and how some of these biblical "times" apply to your role as dad. Some of the easy ones to consider include a time to be born, heal, construct, laugh, cheer, embrace, hold on, mend, speak up, and make peace.

Think about the ways you could take each of these "times" and make them meaningful in the way you interact with your children.

Men have an unhealthy tendency to give up when they believe they have failed. Don't do it. Your children need a dad who works toward engaging with them, so do that instead.

God provided a list of traits that will help you make the jump from intention to reality when harnessing the power of time and the tool of availability. Galatians 5:22–23 (NIV) says, "But the fruit of the Spirit is love, joy, peace, forbearance, kindness, goodness, faithfulness, gentleness and self-control."

When you allow God to make changes in you, then it will transform your role as dad. Your children should be able to see the fruit of your growing relationship with God. What child wouldn't want a dad who is kind, good, faithful, gentle, and self-controlled? Most children will "show and tell" stories of a dad's love, joy, peace, and patience.

The power of prayer is the conversation it initiates between you and God and the change that results from that conversation. Because you want to follow God, it only makes sense to let God know what you're thinking and then read God's Word to discover what He thinks. This combined conversation often results in realigned priorities. You learn to identify the important and adjust the time you spend with the nice but optional so that the important gets the benefit of your attention.

If you feel a sense of guilt because you believe you haven't been spending enough time with your children, don't let that feeling become debilitating. Just start finding more time to advance the cause of moments. These times improve your joy and fill everyone's memory jars. More than a gift to your children, this adjustment will be something you can cherish for the rest of your life.

The promise you have is that this kind of life adjustment will be hard, but God will bring comfort. Second Corinthians 1:4 (MSG) says, "[God] comes alongside us when we go through hard times, and before you know it, he brings us alongside someone else who is going through hard times so that we can be there for that person just as God was there for us." Get comfort—give comfort.

Eye on the Prize

I'm not saying that I have this all together, that I have it made.
But I am well on my way, reaching out for Christ, who has so
wondrously reached out for me. Friends, don't get me wrong: By
no means do I count myself an expert in all of this, but I've got
my eye on the goal, where God is beckoning us onward—
to Jesus. I'm off and running, and I'm not turning back.
PHILIPPIANS 3:12–14 MSG

Limited Supply

Teach us to number our days that
we may get a heart of wisdom.
PSALM 90:12 ESV

Dear God, each day has a value greater than my
understanding, I am sorry for those days when I drift
along as if there is an unlimited supply of time. Help
me use the moments You've given in a way that has
meaning, fulfills purpose, and makes You famous. Amen.

Great Opportunities

*Be very careful, then, how you live—not as unwise
but as wise, making the most of every opportunity,
because the days are evil. Therefore do not be foolish,
but understand what the Lord's will is.*
EPHESIANS 5:15–17 NIV

Dear God, every day has enough bad news. Each day I
live with the consequences of my own sin as well as the
consequences of the sins of others. You ask me to be wise
in the middle of bad days. You want me to identify the
opportunities You send and do something worthwhile
with them. Some of my greatest opportunities are my
children. Help me take the time to invest in them. Amen.

Putting in the Hard Work

*In all labor there is profit, but idle
chatter leads only to poverty.*
PROVERBS 14:23 NKJV

Dear God, being a dad is hard work, but the actual
work results in something so much more valuable
than all the plans and promises that turn to dust in
the wind. Give me strength for the great task
of fatherhood. I am blessed. Amen.

The Time Manager

O LORD, do not be far off!
O you my help, come quickly to my aid!
PSALM 22:19 ESV

Dear God, I could be the greatest time manager the world has ever seen. I could spend more time with my children than any other dad. I could, but without You I would never manage my time in a way that offers the best result. I need You close. I need Your help. Amen.

No-Shame Truth

Concentrate on doing your best for God, work you won't
be ashamed of, laying out the truth plain and simple.
2 TIMOTHY 2:15 MSG

Dear God, my children deserve the truth—Your truth. May I offer You my best by giving them Your best. Help me make Your truth common within the walls of my home. May I never be ashamed to speak Your truth to my children—and to anyone else You send my way. Amen.

What God Would Do

Work willingly at whatever you do, as though you were working for the Lord rather than for people.
COLOSSIANS 3:23 NLT

Dear God, the role of father is something I do for You. As one of Your adopted children, I am asked to take care of my own children in a way that represents Your care. I'm not working to be a good dad in order to win an award from anyone who notices. I am accepting Your help to be a good dad because it's the right way to be a good dad. Amen.

Dad. Overwhelmed.

"Steep your life in God-reality, God-initiative, God-provisions. Don't worry about missing out. You'll find all your everyday human concerns will be met."
MATTHEW 6:33 MSG

Dear God, sometimes being a dad seems to be an overwhelming task. I had never been a dad before my children came into my home. I didn't know what to expect. I'm not always sure how to respond. I can't find the words to describe how stressful this can be. Teach me how to be the dad You want me to be. Would you resolve the concerns I feel? They can be soul crushing. Amen.

Not Good at Waiting

Let us not grow weary while doing good, for in
due season we shall reap if we do not lose heart.
GALATIANS 6:9 NKJV

Dear God, I am planting God seeds in the hearts
of my children. I am not very good at waiting.
Sometimes it seems the time and effort won't add up
to meaningful change. When I am weary, can't seem
to get in step with Your plan, and want to give up—
remind me that You waited on me. May my gratitude
change my perspective on being a dad. Amen.

He Understands Dads

If any of you lacks wisdom, you should ask God,
who gives generously to all without finding fault,
and it will be given to you.
JAMES 1:5 NIV

Dear God, when I don't know what to do, let my prayer
to You be on speed dial. You offer wisdom, and You don't
want me to feel stupid just because I don't understand
what is simple to You. You want me to hunger for wisdom,
and You want me to ask You for understanding. You're not
embarrassed by my questions, and You have the answers
I need. Thanks for understanding dads. Amen.

My Joy

The Power of Living
beyond Circumstance

Douglas didn't initiate a bitter monologue with unsuspecting bystanders, he didn't write a letter to the editor about how his situation merited recognition as martyr of the year, and he didn't plant a root of bitterness that inspired him to binge-watch ad-free mental reruns of his pain years.

Douglas discovered a way to thrive when hard times wore out their welcome. He wanted to live beyond his circumstances, but circumstances kept punching back harder with each unsuccessful movement forward. The secret sauce for Douglas was something the apostle Paul wrote in Philippians 4:11–13 (NIV): "I have learned to be content whatever the circumstances. I know what it is to be in need, and I know what it is to have plenty. I have learned the secret of being content in any and every situation, whether well fed or hungry, whether living in plenty or in want. I can do all this through him who gives me strength."

Contentment is a close companion to joy, and "the joy of the LORD is your strength" (Nehemiah 8:10 NIV). When Douglas lost his wife to long-term illness, lost his job to downsizing, and ultimately faced bankruptcy, it seemed to him that the happiest of days fled to someplace just beyond memory. That's when Douglas made the decision to stop settling for happiness when he could take a soul bath in joy. He discovered that the joy God offered brought contentment because God is *always* in control. The good days, the bad days, and the days of confusion can all be handled by God. Douglas was never forced to face them alone, and God's plans took everything into consideration for the best possible outcome. Why stress out over something God's taken care of?

James 1:2–4 (MSG) reads, "Consider it a sheer gift, friends, when tests and challenges come at you from all sides. You know that under pressure, your faith-life is forced into the open and shows its true colors. So don't try to get out of anything prematurely. Let it do its work so you become mature and well-developed, not deficient in any way."

Think about it this way: good circumstances are generally associated with happiness, bad circumstances are linked to unhappiness, but joy is associated with God's ability to work through *all* circumstances. Maybe that's why Paul could be content in every circumstance. Maybe that's why Douglas discovered joy in difficult circumstances. Maybe that's why you have the opportunity to ditch circumstantial chaos in favor of joy.

Imagine the decrease in anxiety among your children if they see that you don't view every life speedbump as a crisis worthy of immediate panic. Children take their cue from your actions. Your response could be an unintended negative training ground for dealing with life's worst personal headlines.

Joy is one branch from God's love tree. God loved you enough to pay the price for every God law you will ever violate. Restoration is a branch called faith. Faith accepts God's grace. Grace holds out hope. Hope extends joy. Joy fosters contentment. Each of these branches connects in very important ways. The joy you can experience in life's great struggles can be traced back to the love God has always had for you.

Philippians 4:4 (ESV) gives this command: "Rejoice in the Lord always; again I will say, rejoice." This isn't a suggestion based on how you feel or what emotion you might experience in times of gratitude. Like love, joy is a choice. Since this is a command, your feelings have little to do with your obedience.

The rejoicing you offer in response to God's command is a reflection of the gift of joy He's already given. James 1:17 (NIV) says, "Every good and perfect gift is from above, coming down from the Father of the heavenly lights, who does not change like shifting shadows." You don't have to manufacture something that isn't real. All you need to do is rejoice in His good and perfect joy gift.

Douglas hasn't manufactured something from a secret formula. Instead, like Paul, he's simply demonstrating trust in the God who asked him to trust. This truth should leave you echoing Psalm 23:6 (NLT): "Surely your goodness and unfailing love will pursue me all the days of my life, and I will live in the house of the LORD forever." Joy doesn't need to end.

A Full Tank

"As the Father has loved me, so have I loved you. Abide in
my love. If you keep my commandments, you will abide in
my love, just as I have kept my Father's commandments
and abide in his love. These things I have spoken to you,
that my joy may be in you, and that your joy may be full."
JOHN 15:9–11 ESV

On My Way to Eternity

This is the day the LORD has made;
we will rejoice and be glad in it.
PSALM 118:24 NKJV

Dear God, I always thought I had to be happy because
You created another day. Sometimes I don't feel like facing
a new day. Thank You for teaching me to look at today in
a new way. When this moment seems less than amazing,
help me realize I must go through these twenty-four
hours on my way to an eternity with You. The end result
of this day has been worked out because You planned it
that way. So today, I choose to rejoice. Amen.

Hope, Joy, and Peace

I pray that God, the source of hope, will fill you completely with joy and peace because you trust in him.
ROMANS 15:13 NLT

Dear God, if hope is assurance in Your promises, then joy is what I experience when I know Your promises will be kept. Your peace calms my anxieties because with Your guidance everything will just work out. Thanks. Amen.

A Joy Offered

You have turned my mourning into joyful dancing. You have taken away my clothes of mourning and clothed me with joy.
PSALM 30:11 NLT

Dear God, when I bring You sorrow because my dreams have been crushed at the worst possible times, You still offer joy. Even when I don't think my circumstances are changing, joy takes a spare room in my spirit because You keep joy with You wherever You go. Amen.

Find Healing

A joyful heart is good medicine,
but a crushed spirit dries up the bones.
PROVERBS 17:22 ESV

Dear God, my response to everyday life is a matter
of perspective. I can allow my spirit to be crushed
and spend too much time living with a broken spirit,
or I can choose to trust You and find healing in
Your gift of joy. Help me choose joy. Amen.

Love: Given and Accepted

You love him even though you have never seen him.
Though you do not see him now, you trust him;
and you rejoice with a glorious, inexpressible joy.
1 PETER 1:8 NLT

Dear God, I have never seen You, but I have chosen
to accept your love and then love You in return. I can
do this because I trust that everything You said about
redeeming me is true. Knowing that You will work
everything together for my good, I have discovered
joy is both my choice and Your gift. Amen.

Endure the Trials

God's kingdom isn't a matter of what you put in your stomach,
for goodness' sake. It's what God does with your life as he
sets it right, puts it together, and completes it with joy.
ROMANS 14:17 MSG

Dear God, I want to know You more and understand the
way You do things better. So help me endure the trials I
will face today because You promise to right my life, fit
the broken pieces together again, and then complete the
experience with a custom joy meant to change me. Teach
me patience because waiting seems hard. Amen.

Hard Choices

Rejoice in hope, be patient in tribulation,
be constant in prayer.
ROMANS 12:12 ESV

Dear God, over and over again I am confronted with
Your plan to move me to a place of joy. I don't always
understand why it seems joy waits to show up until I
am forced to deal with hard choices. Your Word says
I should rejoice, learn patience, and see prayer as a
regular conversation with You. Amen.

Angels and Impossible Things

*"There is rejoicing in the presence of the
angels of God over one sinner who repents."*
LUKE 15:10 NIV

Dear God, if joy is expressed in what God does in
the middle of seemingly impossible circumstances,
then it shouldn't surprise me that angels express joy
when God's work in the lives of mankind leads to a
rescued life that will one day coexist with angels in
heaven. Thanks for being the God who makes
impossible things possible. Amen.

Share the Source

*The hope of the righteous brings joy,
but the expectation of the wicked will perish.*
PROVERBS 10:28 ESV

Dear God, to be absolutely certain that You have
been, are, and always will be faithful makes the delivery
of joy possible. I have seen people who don't follow
find reasons to be happy, but the wishful thinking they
entertain for their future is a hollow substitute that
will always leave them feeling left out. Help me be
willing to share the source of joy. Amen.

Closer to You

I will shout for joy and sing your praises,
for you have ransomed me.
PSALM 71:23 NLT

Dear God, You've done it—You rescued me. I have been
redeemed from death, and ransomed from the grave. Even
if I die I don't have to be separated from You. I don't have
the words to express everything I feel so either give me
the words or accept my simple gratitude. Joy only works
when I let You initiate, adjust, or allow the circumstances
in my life to bring me closer to You. Amen.

First Line of Inspired Joy

If only you knew how proud I am of you!
I am overwhelmed with joy despite all our troubles.
2 CORINTHIANS 7:4 MSG

Dear God, the apostle Paul expressed to the church in
Corinth what I am learning. In spite of intense personal
trouble he found joy showing up in the lives of people he
was led to help. Let me see my family as a first line of
inspired joy, then my friends, coworkers, and church family.
Let joy mark the soul of this God-rescued dad. Amen.

My Peace

The Power of God's Presence

You are one individual living on a very large planet. This globe is populated with people who have different backgrounds, unique ideas, and big dreams. Since there will be a difference of opinion, there will also be conflict. The conflict can be found in families, among friends, and as the justification for wars between nations. People call for peace, but peace seems the impossible dream.

Maybe peace isn't fully understood. God's Word indicates there is more than one definition for peace. Philippians 4:5–7 (ESV) says, "Let your reasonableness be known to everyone. The Lord is at hand; do not be anxious about anything, but in everything by prayer and supplication with thanksgiving let your requests be made known to God. And the peace of God, which surpasses all understanding, will guard your hearts and your minds in Christ Jesus."

Most people think of peace as an existence without conflict. This is why a serene setting in nature is often thought of as peaceful. God's Word suggests a second definition of peace that is different because, like joy, it can exist in any circumstance. Peace can be experienced even when things aren't peaceful. God wants His people to exist *within* conflict, but *without* the anxiety you might expect from conflict.

You *can* work toward conflict resolution in your home,

and that's what the Bible means when it says, "If it is possible, as far as it depends on you, live at peace with everyone" (Romans 12:18 NIV). However, when conflict exists even after your best efforts fail, then you should allow God's peace to keep anxiety just beyond your reach.

The worry you experience is a faithless expression. You worry because you don't believe God can be trusted to manage your circumstances. When anxiety is high, peace will always be in short supply. Equal parts anxiety and peace will always lead to more anxiety. Worry has to be displaced for peace to have room to grow. Worry grows on its own.

Maybe you've heard stories of men and women who faced incredible trials, yet found themselves wrapped in a peace that made no sense to those around them. This kind of peace is liberated from circumstances. Some people think this outlook is delusional, but people with this kind of peace don't deny the difficulty. Instead, they simply refuse to act rashly on an incomplete picture of their life story.

If Joseph had acted rashly when his brothers sold him as a slave, he might not have been where he needed to be to save his entire family from famine (see Genesis 37, 39–45). On the other hand, because the disciple Peter acted rashly, he often lived with regrets. For example, Peter said he'd never deny Jesus (see Matthew 26:33), but he ran away when trouble came (see Matthew 26:69–75).

For Peter there was no outer peace and no inward peace—only anxiety, broken promises, and denial. Maybe Peter is one guy you can relate to. There might have been times in your life when you had good intentions but caved on promises made. You might have fallen prey to the idea that you could handle a hard circumstance and left the battle sporting a bruised ego because you were out of your league.

Peace can't depend on personal security like safe neighborhoods or ample income. It can't depend on the promises of other people because humans break promises. It can't even depend on avoiding conflict because conflict arrives unscheduled.

Isaiah 26:3 (NKJV) says, "You will keep him in perfect peace, whose mind is stayed on You, because he trusts in You." Peace requires a change in thinking about a God who prefers mercy to justice, grace to unforgiveness, and love to indifference. Peace understands God is for you, stands by you, and "cares for you" (1 Peter 5:7 ESV).

Real peace is found in God's presence. It should not surprise you that when you move away from God, you will struggle to find peace. You can think all the happy thoughts you want, read all the motivational posters ever printed, and post positive quotes on social media, but without God's presence, real peace has moved out of state.

So what's a dad to do? First Peter 3:11 (NLT) says, "Turn away from evil and do good. Search for peace, and work to maintain it."

The Parting Gift

*[Jesus said,] "I'm telling you these things while I'm still
living with you. The Friend, the Holy Spirit whom the Father
will send at my request, will make everything plain to you.
He will remind you of all the things I have told you. I'm
leaving you well and whole. That's my parting gift to you.
Peace. I don't leave you the way you're used to being left—
feeling abandoned, bereft. So don't be upset. Don't be distraught."*
JOHN 14:25–27 MSG

Circumstantial Evidence

*May the God of hope fill you with all joy and
peace in believing, so that by the power of the
Holy Spirit you may abound in hope.*
ROMANS 15:13 ESV

Dear God, since hope is being sure You can be trusted
to keep Your promises, and since joy is assurance that
You can be trusted with all circumstances, and since
peace is a place of comfort no matter the circumstances,
help me rely on Your Spirit to remind me that You
are in control. There will be times I am unsure.
There will be times I forget. Remind me. Amen.

No Separation Anxiety

In peace I will lie down and sleep,
for you alone, O LORD, will keep me safe.
PSALM 4:8 NLT

Dear God, You say that nothing can separate me from
Your love. This is a very comforting thought. When I
lay down tonight, deliver Your comfort and I will be
at peace. You keep me safe, or You take me home.
Either way I win when You're in control. Amen.

The Author of Peace

God is not the author of confusion but of peace.
1 CORINTHIANS 14:33 NKJV

Dear God, I keep hearing that You are confusing,
but Your Word says You didn't write the story
of confusion. You are the author of peace. No
circumstances I will ever encounter are beyond
Your control—and outside Your ability to calm me
down—when anxiety takes aim at my heart. Amen.

In Tune

Let the peace of Christ keep you in tune
with each other, in step with each other.
COLOSSIANS 3:15 MSG

Dear God, when my circumstances are managed by You,
I can trust that You take care of the circumstances of
other Christ followers too. I don't need to compare my
circumstances to others to know that if You can take care
of me, You can also take care of them. Somehow that idea
makes me feel more in tune with those You love. Amen.

Bring Peace—Restore Life

The mind governed by the flesh is death, but the
mind governed by the Spirit is life and peace.
ROMANS 8:6 NIV

Dear God, my human nature takes its temperature
through feelings. Those feelings often lie to me. If I let
those feelings control my actions, I lose. When Your
Spirit is allowed to guide my actions, I discover that,
in the middle of circumstances that leave me drained
emotionally, You can bring peace and restore life. May
I follow You with more than my heart and soul—
let me also follow You with my mind. Amen.

I Accept

*Since we have been justified by faith, we have
peace with God through our Lord Jesus Christ.*
ROMANS 5:1 ESV

Dear God, my accounts are settled with You when I
believe that You provided the only way for my accounts to
be settled. I accept Your rescue. I accept Your forgiveness.
I accept Your love. And because You accept me, I am free
from a spiritual death penalty. Because I believe Jesus was
the only One who could do this—I am at peace. Amen.

Without Conflict

*This righteousness will bring peace. Yes, it
will bring quietness and confidence forever.*
ISAIAH 32:17 NLT

Dear God, let my life be remembered more
for following You than for blazing my own path.
Let my desire be to trust You and obey Your
commands. When I am conflict-free because I
follow You, I look forward to Your peace, improved
composure, and confidence in Your control. Amen.

Wise Peace

The wisdom from above is first of all pure. It is also
peace loving, gentle at all times, and willing to yield
to others. It is full of mercy and the fruit of good
deeds. It shows no favoritism and is always sincere.
JAMES 3:17 NLT

Dear God, Your wisdom demands that I change my
thinking. Your wisdom is pure while my experience is
stained with poor decision-making. Your wisdom is
peace loving and gentle while mine suspects Your plans
are flawed. Your wisdom hinges on mercy while mine is
rigid with justice. Everyone is welcome in Your house
while I show favorites. Let me choose Your wise
peace over my discontent. Amen.

Seek Peace

Depart from evil and do good;
seek peace and pursue it.
PSALM 34:14 NKJV

Dear God, You didn't offer me an "anything goes"
future. You gave me a life plan, You gave me the
assurance of hope, and You want me to accept that
You can manage my life circumstances. Help me
pursue good, seek peace, and follow You. Amen.

My Trust

The Power over Fear

Fear is one of the biggest challenges you face. The topic is negatively fused to the DNA of this book. It leads to spiritual cancer. Fear requires a little room to unpack so you can see it for what it really is—a choice to mistrust God.

There may be reasons you justify the fear you accept, and you can find others who agree that whatever you fear is worth high anxiety. However, God has an option A, and His plan calls for trust.

To be clear, fear indicates that you don't believe God is powerful enough to take care of the things you find fearful. Fear is a take back of trust. Fear wants control but can't find any. Fear makes you think you're alone. Fear causes spiritual amnesia. Fear demands to know things only God knows. Fear removes you from healthy relationships. Fear disrupts meaningful communication with God.

Don't believe you're the only one who's ever spent time hanging out on the corner of Anxiety Avenue and Worry Way. There's no need to extend your stay. Either street is a dead end. King David described an alternative in Psalm 23:1–5 (MSG): "GOD, my shepherd! I don't need a thing. You have bedded me down in lush meadows, you find me quiet pools to drink from. True to your word, you let me catch my breath and send me in the right direction. Even when the way goes through Death Valley, I'm not afraid when you walk at my side. Your trusty shepherd's crook makes me feel secure. You serve me a six-course dinner right in front of my enemies. You revive my drooping head; my cup brims with blessing."

You might not want to be compared with sheep, but that's what God does in scripture. Sheep are anxious creatures, and like sheep, you too live with a fear you attempt to hide. Like sheep, you wander away from the Shepherd. You try to figure things out without bothering God. You're certain you can manage on your own. Stop it. The God of the universe *never* said, *"Don't bother me with your problems, I'm too busy. Figure life out on your own. If you come to me broken and bruised it's not like you weren't warned."* No, God knew you would need help. Psalm 55:22 (NIV) says, "Cast your cares on the LORD." He guides. He protects. He meets needs. He is strong. He is mighty. Trust Him.

Jesus, the Good Shepherd, sent this comforting word picture through John 10:27 (NLT): "My sheep listen to my voice; I know them, and they follow me." He knows what you need and how to match that need with His ability to provide. *Trust Him.*

Fear is easy—trust is not. Whenever fear threatens to take you to the mat, remember Psalm 56:3–4 (NKJV): "Whenever I am afraid, I will trust in You. In God (I will praise His word), in God I have put my trust; I will not fear. What can flesh do to me?" This is not a psalm of false bravado or wishful thinking. Instead, this is a passage of scripture that drives home the point that, even in your worst-case scenario, your trust in God remains a superior choice to fear.

If you need more assurance, keep reading. Romans

8:38–39 (ESV) says, "I am sure that neither death nor life, nor angels nor rulers, nor things present nor things to come, nor powers, nor height nor depth, nor anything else in all creation, will be able to separate us from the love of God in Christ Jesus our Lord." God's love is assured. His promises are unfailing. His control is without meaningful challenge. God is much bigger than your fear.

Fear disrupts everything in your Christian life. Without trust in God you can't believe His promises, accept His gifts, or share His love. Without trust you will be suspicious, resist close friendships, and embrace sarcasm while searching for evidence that the world really is as bad as you think. *Trust Him.*

When society suggests fear is the only response, they overlook option A. Romans 12:2 (NIV) says, "Do not conform to the pattern of this world, but be transformed by the renewing of your mind. Then you will be able to test and approve what God's will is—his good, pleasing and perfect will." Part of a transformed life is an intolerance of fear made possible by a decision to trust Him.

You're Safe

You who sit down in the High God's presence, spend the night in Shaddai's shadow, say this: "God, you're my refuge. I trust in you and I'm safe!" That's right—he rescues you from hidden traps, shields you from deadly hazards. His huge outstretched arms protect you—under them you're perfectly safe; his arms fend off all harm. Fear nothing—not wild wolves in the night, not flying arrows in the day, not disease that prowls through the darkness, not disaster that erupts at high noon.
PSALM 91:1–5 MSG

Seeking Answers

*Trust in the Lord with all your heart;
do not depend on your own understanding.*
PROVERBS 3:5 NLT

Dear God, the way I think can lead me to wrong conclusions, to act on wrong information, and to seek answers in wrong thinking. Let my trust in You lead me to Your conclusions by using Your wisdom, understanding, and plan. Amen.

Keep Me Steadfast

They will have no fear of bad news;
their hearts are steadfast, trusting in the LORD.
PSALM 112:7 NIV

Dear God, when I hear the news and it sounds bad, help me remember that in the end You win, in the present You guide my steps, and in time I will become more like You—when I trust that Your best for me is really "best for me." Keep me steadfast. Keep me trusting. Amen.

The Trouble Pile

Pile your troubles on GOD's shoulders—he'll carry your load,
he'll help you out. He'll never let good people topple into ruin.
PSALM 55:22 MSG

Dear God, my shoulders seem big to my children, but they are small compared to Yours. My heaviest load is light to You. My troubles never throw You off balance. I am constantly grateful that You actually want to help me. Amen.

Remove My Dread

"Do not fear, for I am with you; do not be dismayed,
for I am your God. I will strengthen you and help you;
I will uphold you with my righteous right hand."
ISAIAH 41:10 NIV

Dear God, if I don't experience fear I can easily experience
dread. It can be a feeling of doom that can sidetrack me
from looking to You. In those moments, remind me that
You strengthen, You help, and Your hand alone is strong
enough to remove my dread and erase my fear. Amen.

I Am Safe

Fearing people is a dangerous trap,
but trusting the LORD means safety.
PROVERBS 29:25 NLT

Dear God, when I care too much about what other
people think, help me remember that You call this a
trap. It's a trap compared to the time I invest paying
attention to what You think. When I am used to
walking among other people in fear, help me
remember with You I am safe. Amen.

When I Am Overwhelmed

*Do not be anxious about anything, but in everything
by prayer and supplication with thanksgiving
let your requests be made known to God.*
PHILIPPIANS 4:6 ESV

Dear God, You have made it absolutely clear that
anxiety, concern, and fear distract me from trusting
You. When I am overwhelmed, bring my heart to You
in prayer and let me lay down all the things that keep
me from thinking about You. I need Your help. Thanks
for thinking of my needs as important. Amen.

Unnecessary—Unhealthy

*The LORD is my light and my salvation—
so why should I be afraid? The LORD is my fortress,
protecting me from danger, so why should I tremble?*
PSALM 27:1 NLT

Dear God, when life is dark and I need rescue, help me
remember my first response should be trust, not fear. You
can protect me from danger. I know this is true, but there
are times when my heart is weak within me. Help me
remember fear is an unnecessary and unhealthy condition.
Cause my feet to run to You and my heart to rejoice when
You show the way through each fearful moment. Amen.

The Latest What-If

"Don't get worked up about what may or may not happen tomorrow. God will help you deal with whatever hard things come up when the time comes."
MATTHEW 6:34 MSG

Dear God, help me avoid the dangerous game of "what if." Playing this game means I spend more time thinking about what might happen instead of trusting Your wisdom in dealing with each new difficulty. When my mind gravitates to the latest what-if, help me remember nothing will ever happen that You can't deal with. Amen.

A Shortened Life

"Can all your worries add a single moment to your life?"
MATTHEW 6:27 NLT

Dear God, if humans could live a little longer just by worrying, then why don't we live longer? It seems that worry and stress actually shorten life. So why do I welcome worry to my thinking? It can't save me, it can't calm me, and it can't make people like me more. Thanks for the reminder that fear doesn't enhance my life. Amen.

In Every Circumstance

The LORD is near to the brokenhearted
and saves the crushed in spirit.
PSALM 34:18 ESV

Dear God, You don't abandon me when my spirit is riddled with wounds and my heart has been fractured. It doesn't even matter if the damage is my fault or the fault of someone else. You take the fear that caused the wounds and offer to replace it with friendship. Because I am broken, help me trust You in every circumstance. Amen.

―――――――――――――

An Insignificant Speck?

"Do not fear therefore; you are of
more value than many sparrows."
MATTHEW 10:31 NKJV

Dear God, I can feel like an insignificant speck on this big blue marble. You created the heavens and the earth, but sometimes I feel I am insignificant in comparison. It's easy to believe You have more important things to do than listen to my struggles. But You feed sparrows. You pay attention when one of them dies. If sparrows are worth Your notice, help me remember You want to hear from me. I never need to fear that I am alone. Amen.

My Work

The Power of Provision

Wayne was a small-town mechanic. His tools were used for more than forty years to get people back on the road. Then in the early 1980s he retired. In between his first day and his last, Wayne completed each day's work by the sweat of his brow. With every connection between wrench and bolt, with every carburetor adjustment, and with every new seal, Wayne did his best to satisfy the expectations of his boss and customers. More than that, Wayne knew his skills could be used to provide for his wife and three daughters.

When he wasn't elbow deep in engine parts, Wayne fed his chickens, cultivated a half-acre garden, and filled his potato cellar for winter. He understood the value of hard work and never seemed to complain. Like most men of his era, Wayne saw being able to provide as a privilege. From the moment Wayne said "I do" to his wife, he welcomed work as a part of the promise he made to her. He made that promise when he repeated these vows to her: "to have and to hold from this day forward, for better, for worse, for richer, for poorer, in sickness and in health, until death do us part."

Every morning when the sun coaxed him from slumber and work extended a daily summons, Wayne rose, worked, and carved out a life for his family. There were days he might not have been especially interested in why a customer's vehicle made a certain sound when the customer drove on dirt roads, but the work was less daily drudgery and more promise fulfillment.

Proverbs 12:11 (NLT) says, "A hard worker has plenty of food, but a person who chases fantasies has no sense." God commends people who work hard. God says work is a good thing.

One of the reasons God urges work is found in Acts 20:35 (NIV), where Paul says, "By this kind of hard work we must help the weak, remembering the words the Lord Jesus himself said: 'It is more blessed to give than to receive.'" Your hard work can be used to bless others who are living in a time of personal struggle. The proceeds of your hard work can be used by God to meet their needs as a tangible demonstration of the love God shares with you. For Wayne, that meant sending garden produce or eggs home with family, friends, and neighbors.

Work may seem like a means to an end. You may find yourself working for the weekend, phoning it in, or attempting to lower the expectations of your boss. Yet God is clear about who you work for in Ephesians 6:6–7 (MSG): "Don't just do what you have to do to get by, but work heartily, as Christ's servants doing what God wants you to do. And work with a smile on your face, always keeping in mind that no matter who happens to be giving the orders, you're really serving God."

The time you spend representing Jesus doesn't stop when you begin and end a weekend worship service. Your work represents the character and quality of the God you serve. Work is important for many different reasons, but it is not something to be avoided—or overindulged.

As a dad you find yourself working to take care of

finances for your family, but if you spend so much time working that you don't have much left for your children, then work has moved from something that takes care of your family's needs to something that has become more important than family. First Corinthians 10:24 (MSG) says, "We want to live well, but our foremost efforts should be to help others live well." You want your children to live well. That requires your involvement. The extra money brought home by a workaholic can't make a down payment on the time you missed with your children.

Back in the beginning, when Adam and Eve sinned and were removed from the Garden of Eden, God gave Adam something that would help keep him from trouble. Although it didn't seem like it at the time, God's gift to Adam was work (see Genesis 3:17–19 and Colossians 3:23–24).

You likely know someone like Wayne. Maybe you *are* someone like Wayne. You don't have to be a Christ follower to have a good work ethic, but being a Christian provides additional purpose, motivation, and reason for hard work. When you work, work hard. When you're home, engage well. When you help others, serve willingly.

Whatever He Does

*Blessed is the man who walks not in the counsel of
the ungodly, nor stands in the path of sinners, nor sits
in the seat of the scornful; but his delight is in the law
of the LORD, and in His law he meditates day and
night. He shall be like a tree planted by the rivers of
water, that brings forth its fruit in its season, whose leaf
also shall not wither; and whatever he does shall prosper.*
PSALM 1:1–3 NKJV

Make a Difference

*Whatever you do, in word or deed,
do everything in the name of the Lord Jesus.*
COLOSSIANS 3:17 ESV

Dear God, when I read that everything I do is completed
as Your representative, I have to admit that if I really
believe this is true, then there have been days I am
ashamed of my work conduct. Help me remember that
people watch me to see if You really make a difference.
May I allow You to make a difference through me. Amen.

No Ineffective Ants

*You lazy fool, look at an ant. Watch it closely; let it teach
you a thing or two. Nobody has to tell it what to do. All
summer it stores up food; at harvest it stockpiles provisions.*
PROVERBS 6:6–8 MSG

Dear God, I think You instill within every man the desire
to care for his family. I don't need to wonder if it's the
right thing to do, I just need to do it. You have promised
me a future that connects with Your plan and then given
me the desire to bring my family with me. Help me learn
from You so the desire to take care of my family doesn't
weaken and become ineffective. Amen.

Family-Changing Care

*Those who won't care for their relatives, especially
those in their own household, have denied the true
faith. Such people are worse than unbelievers.*
1 TIMOTHY 5:8 NLT

Dear God, while You give me a desire to care for my
family, I know I must be a full partner with that desire.
Help me care for my family in a way that shows others
that walking with You makes a positive difference. As far
as it depends on me, help me do the work that places the
needs of my family above personal interests. Amen.

The Ultimate Boss

*Be steadfast, immovable, always abounding in the work of the
Lord, knowing that your labor is not in vain in the Lord.*
1 CORINTHIANS 15:58 NKJV

Dear God, I know I work for You. I am certain that
no matter who signs my check, they are not really my
ultimate boss. Work is sacred to You, so help me treat
what I do as a gift to the One I serve. The work You
give provides for my family, keeps me active, and is
an expression of Your gift to me. Amen.

In the Path of People

*"Take courage! Do not let your hands be weak,
for your work shall be rewarded."*
2 CHRONICLES 15:7 ESV

Dear God, You create work to benefit community.
More than me, more than my wife, and more than my
children, You have given me something that puts me in
the path of people who need to know You. My work is
not just an exercise in self-fulfillment. Instead, it is daily
testimony to my employer and the people I help. Amen.

Work Is a Blessing

*I went past the field of a sluggard, past the vineyard of someone
who has no sense; thorns had come up everywhere, the ground
was covered with weeds, and the stone wall was in ruins.*
PROVERBS 24:30–31 NIV

Dear God, I am certain that work is a blessing to
me and my family. As long as I am able, help me use
the skills You've given me to provide for my family and
help where I can. When I feel like abandoning work,
there is always a price to pay. I don't want my family
to pay that bill. Send help when I need it—give
me strength for each new day. Amen.

═══════════════

The Foreman

*Put GOD in charge of your work,
then what you've planned will take place.*
PROVERBS 16:3 MSG

Dear God, you know what I need. I want you to be the
foreman of my work schedule. Show me what needs to be
done, and give me the wisdom to do it. When the plans
I've made connect with the job you want me to do, may I
recognize the blessing of working with You. Amen.

Hired to Do a Job

One who is slack in his work is
brother to one who destroys.
PROVERBS 18:9 NIV

Dear God, there are times when I know I'm not
giving 100 percent. When the work is too hard and it
seems easier just to relax, help me remember that my
employer provides an income for the work I do, and I
am dishonest when I don't do that work. Amen.

All That I Do

Let all that you do be done in love.
1 CORINTHIANS 16:14 ESV

Dear God, I can work all day long, I can work the
weekends, and I can work holidays, but if what I do isn't
motivated by love, then I'm just an employee and not Your
representative. Help me make the choice to demonstrate
kind love in the workplace just like I choose to show it to
my family. Let those I work with and those in my home
see the difference love makes in me. Amen.

My Finances

The Power of a Manager

There is nothing that has been made that was made without first using something God created. He gave you lungs to breathe air, which He provided. He gave you eyes to see, ears to hear, and a mind to understand the things you actually see and hear, and He just keeps on giving. He wants you to do something with His gifts.

Is it possible that God's gifts are meant to be shared? Is it reasonable to suggest that God wants to multiply the value of every one of His gifts? Is it conceivable that God can use you to share His gifts?

This type of gift management is like filling a cup with water and then continuing to pour even after the cup overflows. The cup remains full, but the overflow touches everything around it. The opposite view is like owning an artesian well you use to quench your thirst, but never sharing because you are concerned that if you let others drink, you will never have enough for yourself.

The apostle Paul wrote in Philippians 4:19 (MSG), "You can be sure that God will take care of everything you need, his generosity exceeding even yours in the glory that pours from Jesus."

When you really grab hold of the truth that God will take care of your *needs*, you can stop treating Him like a genie that should grant your immediate *wants*. Knowing that God can be trusted with your needs makes it easier to share His gifts with others. Believing that God takes care of you means God's gift was accepted. Romans 8:32 (NIV) says, "He who did not spare his own Son, but gave him up for us all—how will he not also, along with him, graciously give us all things?"

Since God uses a variety of ways to ensure you have what you need, He asks you to manage His gifts. First Peter 4:10 (NLT) says, "God has given each of you a gift from his great variety of spiritual gifts. Use them well to serve one another."

This is a compatible concept to a parable Jesus taught about stewardship. You can read that parable in Matthew 25. An employer gave three managers large sums of money to invest while he was away on business. The money was not theirs to keep but to use to increase their employer's financial portfolio. The first two men invested and doubled their employer's cash before he returned. The third man? Well, he buried the money and waited anxiously for the boss to return. He didn't want to disappoint his employer by losing money.

This third manager didn't invest because his fear talked him out of obedience. When the boss returned, he commended the first two men for being wise with the use of his money. He was much less enthusiastic about the third man. The boss suggested that if the man had done nothing more than put the money in the bank, at least he would have been able to show interest instead of a lack of initiative.

God asks you to manage the resources He's given to you. This includes managing your children, the needs of your family, love, mercy, kindness, and forgiveness. The list is much longer, but this is a good start. In Luke 16:10 (NIV),

Jesus talks about the faithfulness of those who manage: "Whoever can be trusted with very little can also be trusted with much, and whoever is dishonest with very little will also be dishonest with much."

What Jesus seems to be warning against is living for spiritual "gold stars" and clubhouse attaboys then insisting on calling it faithfulness. Jesus was speaking to, and about, the religious leaders of the time. They had turned religion into a who's who list of men who thought they were spiritually superior. Jesus said this way of thinking made them less faithful and increasingly dishonest. They had substituted a relationship with God for playing the role of the spiritually smug. They wanted other humans to admire their rule keeping but refused to let God change their hearts. They were investing in a nongift.

What does all this mean? Everything you have can be traced to the hand of a loving God. He wants you to faithfully manage His gifts. He will take care of your needs, but He needs you to be responsible with what He provides. Your faithfulness in managing what He gives is an expression of worship to Him.

A Body of Management

*Didn't you realize that your body is a sacred place, the place
of the Holy Spirit? Don't you see that you can't live however
you please, squandering what God paid such a high price
for? The physical part of you is not some piece of property
belonging to the spiritual part of you. God owns the whole
works. So let people see God in and through your body.*
1 CORINTHIANS 6:19–20 MSG

Uniquely Fit

All things should be done decently and in order.
1 CORINTHIANS 14:40 ESV

Dear God, when I feel like "winging it," remind
me that Your plans for me are served up with clarity,
purpose, and order. When my willingness to obey is in
line with Your willingness to lead, that's when it will
be most clear that Your plan is perfectly designed
and uniquely fit for me. Help me learn to obey with
the attitude of one who's willing. Amen.

The Cost Analysis

"Don't begin until you count the cost. For who would
begin construction of a building without first calculating
the cost to see if there is enough money to finish it?"
Luke 14:28 nlt

Dear God, I'd like to think I'd never be the guy who
throws myself into a project without having some idea
of what I will face, but I have done so and probably will
again. Help me learn to count the cost of each decision
so that, when I agree to do something, I will be
better able to keep my promise. Amen.

A Dad of Integrity

A good name is more desirable than great riches;
to be esteemed is better than silver or gold.
Proverbs 22:1 niv

Dear God, there is one thing I can use to help me
in life and that's a good reputation. It's best to keep a
good reputation, but it can also be rebuilt—it just takes
longer. Help me stand for You and may that reputation
tell others that You are worth serving. Amen.

Opportunity versus Scheme

The plans of the diligent lead surely to abundance,
but everyone who is hasty comes only to poverty.
PROVERBS 21:5 ESV

Dear God, help me avoid get-rich-quick ideas. I absolutely
want to take advantage of the opportunities You bring
my way, but I don't want to compromise a right standing
with You for a few extra bucks. May my hard work
and Your opportunities lead to a life that meets the
needs of my family and leaves my heart in the
company of my King. Amen.

Stopping Points

Moderation is better than muscle,
self-control better than political power.
PROVERBS 16:32 MSG

Dear God, help me resist fighting for position and
power if the outcome will remove me from Your will
and cause hurt to my family. May my drive to succeed
be filled with checkpoints where I can evaluate my
motives and revisit Your plans. It is too easy for me
to think the life I live here is more important than
the life I will one day live with You. Amen.

What's Mine Is Yours

Honor the LORD with your possessions.
PROVERBS 3:9 NKJV

Dear God, what's mine is Yours because what's
Yours is mine when I become part of Your family.
You call that grace. I couldn't live without all the
things You give to me. May this truth instill a heart
of gratitude that chooses to honor You with my time,
my talent, and my money. Amen.

Skill, Strength, and Purpose

*"Remember the LORD your God. He is the
one who gives you power to be successful."*
DEUTERONOMY 8:18 NLT

Dear God, my skill, my strength, and my purpose all
come from You. When I successfully follow Your plan,
it is Your power that leads me to that success. Every
achievement that has any real meaning comes from Your
thinking and is part of Your purpose. Thank You. Amen.

Adapt My Plans

A man's heart plans his way,
but the LORD directs his steps.
PROVERBS 16:9 NKJV

Dear God, I can plan my ways and steps wherever I
want, but this choice will never get me as far as if I let
You lead me in any direction You want—even when
I've made other plans. If I'm to be a good manager for
my family, and with Your resources, it means I will
need to adapt my plans to fit Your purpose. Amen.

―――――――――――――

More Than Manage

Be careful how you live. Don't live
like fools, but like those who are wise.
EPHESIANS 5:15 NLT

Dear God, don't let me play the fool when it comes to
the choices I make about how to live. A fool has no
plans, accepts no purpose, and assumes little responsibility.
Help me manage my time, decisions, and resources in a
way that reflects a belief that You really matter. Amen.

What I Don't Need

"Guard against every kind of greed.
Life is not measured by how much you own."
LUKE 12:15 NLT

Dear God, help me be content with what You give me.
Give me much or give me little, but never let me think
that what I have defines who I am. When greed threatens
to infect my choices, help me resist the immediate in
favor of my future with You. If You want me to manage
what I have, maybe You want me to manage without
things I don't really need. Amen.

No Napping

Keep a cool head. Stay alert. The Devil is poised to pounce,
and would like nothing better than to catch you napping. Keep
your guard up. You're not the only ones plunged into these hard
times. It's the same with Christians all over the world.
1 PETER 5:8–9 MSG

Dear God, when I fail to manage Your resources and
my time, I leave myself open to attack from a great
enemy. Let me stop sleeping on the job. Help me
protect what You've given me to take care of
because it ultimately is Yours. Amen.

My Church

The Power of Christian Family

If the church is the body of Christ, then the church can't be confined to a building. The body of Christ is composed of people living town to town, country to country, and continent to continent. God's church is global, and you won't be able to meet everyone in a lifetime. That's one of the benefits of eternity.

The primary benefit of a church building is providing a place where people can gather to encourage and be encouraged, pray and praise, share and serve. God wants that to happen. Hebrews 10:24–25 (NLT) says, "Let us think of ways to motivate one another to acts of love and good works. And let us not neglect our meeting together, as some people do, but encourage one another, especially now that the day of his return is drawing near."

Can you follow God and never visit a church building? Maybe, but your spiritual growth is stunted when you choose to be a spiritual loner. You don't get to heaven by having a perfect attendance record, but you make your life on earth more defeating by keeping your family at a distance.

You might believe that people who gather in church buildings on the weekend are hypocrites. You've seen them sing in church and then take advantage of people during the week. You've heard words of praise one day and gossip around the watercooler the next. You've seen them on their best behavior and witnessed their worst moments. Why spend time with people like that?

If you're honest, your own actions are not in perfect alignment with God's expectations either. The gathering of family in a church building is not a collection of the perfect, nor an exhibition of the spiritually elite. Church is a place where strugglers discover second chances, seekers find answers, and mature believers inspire those who struggle and seek because they have both sought and struggled.

Perfection doesn't exist outside the walls of a church building. It doesn't exist inside either. Be encouraged. You don't gather with Christian superheroes, you gather with fellow humans who wrestle with choices, and sometimes make the wrong ones. The church can be a collection of imperfect humans who agree to walk together in God's great adventure.

Family reunions feature tension, so why should you expect to attend church without the potential for similar drama? Don't run away, hide, or feel intimidated. First John 4:7–8 (MSG) gives great advice on dealing with difficult Christians: "My beloved friends, let us continue to love each other since love comes from God. Everyone who loves is born of God and experiences a relationship with God. The person who refuses to love doesn't know the first thing about God, because God is love—so you can't know him if you don't love."

When you love with the love of God, out-of-sync Christians find cause to reconsider community. Get your eyes off the distractions and realize everyone in the room simply needs more Jesus. When the room is filled with worshippers, there is a mutual recognition that the only

One with absolute perfection is always the most important focal point in the room.

Romans 12:3 (NIV) says, "For by the grace given me I say to every one of you: Do not think of yourself more highly than you ought, but rather think of yourself with sober judgment, in accordance with the faith God has distributed to each of you." God's grace gift insists you remember what He's done for you. What He's done is to rescue you when you couldn't rescue yourself. It's hard to brag about yourself when you're admitting you need help.

God made everyone seated in the sanctuary with different personalities, interests, and character traits. Somehow He wants all these different people to work together in His name to do what seems impossible—spread His love to people who have different personalities, interests, and character traits. The future He's planned will need just such people. You will too.

God never promised there would be perfectly sinless believers. It just isn't possible this side of heaven. If you've trusted Jesus as your soul rescuer, then you are being made into a new creation—just like those in your church family. Walk together without comparing merit badges. God never does.

Offenses Forgiven

So, chosen by God for this new life of love, dress in the wardrobe God picked out for you: compassion, kindness, humility, quiet strength, discipline. Be even-tempered, content with second place, quick to forgive an offense. Forgive as quickly and completely as the Master forgave you. And regardless of what else you put on, wear love. It's your basic, all-purpose garment. Never be without it.
COLOSSIANS 3:12–14 MSG

═══════════════════

Comparison Confusion

Live in harmony with each other. Let there be no divisions in the church. Rather, be of one mind, united in thought and purpose.
1 CORINTHIANS 1:10 NLT

Dear God, when I pay more attention to who I serve with, rather than who I am serving, help me remember I can become distracted by the urge to compare myself with others. You want Your family to work together. Help me stop comparing spiritual scars and stop competing for a more impressive Christian life highlight reel. Amen.

Equal Access

This mystery is that the Gentiles are fellow heirs,
members of the same body, and partakers of the
promise in Christ Jesus through the gospel.
EPHESIANS 3:6 ESV

Dear God, I am grateful that You sent Your Son,
Jesus, for all people. Your rescue plan covered those
willing to be rescued—without exclusion. I am promised
the companionship of Your Spirit, the rescue of Your Son,
and Your personal attention when I pray. Those who are
rescued are part of my spiritual family, and we all have
equal access to You. Thanks for refusing to leave anyone
out of Your plan or away from Your love. Amen.

Spiritual Family

Long, long ago he decided to adopt us
into his family through Jesus Christ.
EPHESIANS 1:5 MSG

Dear God, Your plan for Your people was connection
through a spiritual family. You designed us to need
You and need each other in this family of the believing.
You take people like me who never deserved Your love
and gave us adoption papers that welcomed us into Your
family. By accepting this incredible gift I experience
something I could never earn, I didn't deserve, and was
more than I could hope for—rescue from my own
sin. I am honored to be Your child. Amen.

The One—The Only

There is one body and one Spirit, just as you were
called to one hope when you were called; one Lord,
one faith, one baptism; one God and Father of all,
who is over all and through all and in all.
Ephesians 4:4–6 niv

Dear God, You are the author of one. You don't want
Your family divided so You command us to be one.
You offer belief as the way to God, and there is only
one You. When I understand that You don't change
Your offer of rescue based on who You are dealing with,
then I can relax knowing You are the same yesterday,
today, and forever. In You I am secure. Amen.

Power of Community

To the church of God which is at Corinth, to those
who are sanctified in Christ Jesus, called to be saints,
with all who in every place call on the name of
Jesus Christ our Lord, both theirs and ours.
1 Corinthians 1:2 nkjv

Dear God, from one group of believers in Corinth to
the Christ followers I share life with today, You made
sure Your Word clearly demonstrates that those You've
rescued are no longer alone. They are part of a community
of believers who should be able to rely on each other.
I am grateful to have the power of community
in my journey with You. Amen.

Bigger Than My Interests

All of you together are Christ's body,
and each of you is a part of it.
1 CORINTHIANS 12:27 NLT

Dear God, the way You describe the church or body of Christ is not a place of halfhearted friendships and whole-hearted dread at the thought of participating. The body of Christ is made up of people like me, and we are better when we work together. Remind me that I am a part of something bigger than my own interests. Amen.

Intentional Resistance

He who is in you is greater than he who is in the world.
1 JOHN 4:4 ESV

Dear God, You call Your Spirit a helper, counselor, and guide. When I accepted Your rescue plan, something greater than the one who seeks to sabotage Your plans was placed deep in the center of what makes me, me. Satan can't thwart Your plans for me without permission. Use my Christian family to help me resist plans that are never for my good. Amen.

Community of the Faithful

He handed out gifts of apostle, prophet, evangelist, and pastor-teacher to train Christ's followers in skilled servant work, working within Christ's body, the church, until we're all moving rhythmically and easily with each other, efficient and graceful in response to God's Son, fully mature adults, fully developed within and without, fully alive like Christ.
EPHESIANS 4:11–13 MSG

Dear God, You've given me a gift that I am to use to help the community of the faithful. Help me recognize that others within Your church are also learning to share their gifts. Help us take those gifts and make them useful to You so You can make changes in us and in those who watch us grow. Amen.

Walking in Step

There is therefore now no condemnation to those who are in Christ Jesus, who do not walk according to the flesh, but according to the Spirit.
ROMANS 8:1 NKJV

Dear God, in the company of Your family, I can learn to walk in step with Your Spirit. When I keep to myself, I make decisions that were never Your plan for me. I sleep better when I keep Your Spirit as my travel companion. When I have brothers who join me, the journey just gets better. Amen.

Living Disengaged

If one member suffers, all suffer together;
if one member is honored, all rejoice together.
1 CORINTHIANS 12:26 ESV

Dear God, there is a connection among those who
worship together. I want to grab hold of the idea that
these men and women are brothers and sisters in Your
family. Their good news should be celebrated, and their
bad news should be reason for sympathy. Stop me from
living disengaged among Your family. Amen.

Understand the Connection

No more lies, no more pretense. Tell your neighbor the truth.
In Christ's body we're all connected to each other, after all.
EPHESIANS 4:25 MSG

Dear God, sometimes it's easier to try to do things on
my own. It's even easy to ignore my Christian family
and the people who live close to me because I'm busy
with my own little world. You have truth and want me
to share it. I need to understand the connection You
want me to have with others so that, when I share Your
truth, it comes from the heart of a friend and not
someone they aren't sure even cares. Amen.

My Ministry

The Power of Purpose

Purpose is the *why* behind day-to-day living. Purpose presents the case for getting out of bed in the morning. Purpose says there's a job to do and you're the one to get it done. Do you know your purpose? You have one.

Some people settle for a *reason* instead of a *purpose*. You might think that the reason you exist is because your parents had a son, the reason for living is a mystery, or the reason you get up is to earn a living.

Purpose and reason are always vying for your allegiance. Purpose is a gift given to you by God, but a reason is often personal justification for struggling through another day. Purpose offers a blueprint for life while reason is only interested in dealing with immediate disasters. Purpose is a long view, and a reason can't wait for the weekend.

Maybe you've settled for a reason for living while never giving your life purpose much thought. What does purpose look like? Ephesians 1:11–12 (MSG) says, "It's in Christ that we find out who we are and what we are living for. Long before we first heard of Christ and got our hopes up, he had his eye on us, had designs on us for glorious living, part of the overall purpose he is working out in everything and everyone."

If your heart responds to the idea of knowing who you are, God having His eye on you, and knowing He designed you for glorious living, then maybe you are still looking for your purpose. Maybe the *reasons* you've accepted have an unappealing patina.

Reasons play it safe. Purpose encourages you to take a plunge into the deep end. Purpose doesn't always seem safe, it may not seem practical, and it never promises wealth, status, or fame. Purpose is a God-given calling to make the most of the relatively short time you're here on earth. It has eternal significance, exercises a role of godly influence, and is often called ministry.

Ministry sounds like something that only happens in church or a soup kitchen, or working with people who don't speak your language. Ministry *can* be these things, but it always includes your family and the people you come in contact with each day.

If you've ever been curious about God's interest in you, consider Psalm 139:13–16 (msg), which says, "Oh yes, you shaped me first inside, then out; you formed me in my mother's womb. I thank you, High God—you're breathtaking! Body and soul, I am marvelously made! I worship in adoration—what a creation! You know me inside and out, you know every bone in my body; you know exactly how I was made, bit by bit, how I was sculpted from nothing into something. Like an open book, you watched me grow from conception to birth; all the stages of my life were spread out before you, the days of my life all prepared before I'd even lived one day."

The ministry God wants to do through you starts with understanding that He intentionally created you. You're here on purpose. You matter to God. He made the choice to love you before you were born and planned for your future even if you never loved Him in return. If that's the best news you've heard all day, then share it. Telling others about God's great rescue is always the start of your ministry and plays a primary role in your purpose.

God chose to give lawbreakers a purpose and made it clear in Ephesians 2:1–5 (NLT): "Once you were dead because of your disobedience and your many sins. You used to live in sin, just like the rest of the world, obeying the devil—the commander of the powers in the unseen world. He is the spirit at work in the hearts of those who refuse to obey God. All of us used to live that way, following the passionate desires and inclinations of our sinful nature. By our very nature we were subject to God's anger, just like everyone else.

"But God is so rich in mercy, and he loved us so much, that even though we were dead because of our sins, he gave us life when he raised Christ from the dead. (It is only by God's grace that you have been saved!)"

Grace + purpose = life that's really life.

Go and Train

Jesus, undeterred, went right ahead and gave his charge:
"God authorized and commanded me to commission you:
Go out and train everyone you meet, far and near, in this
way of life, marking them by baptism in the threefold name:
Father, Son, and Holy Spirit. Then instruct them in the
practice of all I have commanded you. I'll be with you as you
do this, day after day after day, right up to the end of the age."
MATTHEW 28:18–20 MSG

What You Want Me to Do

Fear God and keep his commandments,
for this is the whole duty of man.
ECCLESIASTES 12:13 ESV

Dear God, if the greatest purpose is to experience
awe when I think of You, help me think of You more.
If my greatest duty is to follow Your commands, then
help me learn more about what You want me to do.
Help me understand my purpose and then adjust
my decisions to cooperate with You. Amen.

Moving in God's Direction

Since we are surrounded by such a great cloud of witnesses,
let us throw off everything that hinders and the sin
that so easily entangles. And let us run with
perseverance the race marked out for us.

HEBREWS 12:1 NIV

Dear God, runners have a course marked off for them to
follow. When they leave the course to follow their own
interpretation of the path, they get off course. Comparing
my choice to follow You with running causes me to
wonder how often I've gotten off track because I stopped
following directions. When sin grabs at my journey feet,
and I find myself tripped up, help me get back on my
feet and get moving—in Your direction. Amen.

Lead Me to Purpose

Here's what I want you to do, God helping you:
Take your everyday, ordinary life—your sleeping,
eating, going-to-work, and walking-around life—
and place it before God as an offering.

ROMANS 12:1 MSG

Dear God, I don't want to hold anything back from You.
When I say that I want You to be in control of my life,
then I need help keeping my tongue from trying to tell
You how to run things. You have a purpose for me so I
need to allow You to take the circumstances, the moments,
the appetites, and my work and home life, and let You
make the choices that lead me to purpose. Amen.

Bigger Than Suggestions

Don't become so well-adjusted to your culture that you fit into it without even thinking. Instead, fix your attention on God.
ROMANS 12:2 MSG

Dear God, why is it so easy to shift my focus from following You to pleasing other people? It is natural to step back from firm resolutions to follow You with every part of me in order to step forward to something I know You don't want for me—just because a friend or coworker suggests it's a good idea. Let me focus on You and say no every time I need to when someone suggests a walk-away plan. Your purpose for me is so much bigger than any shortsighted suggestion. Amen.

You Called. I Answered.

Each person should live as a believer in whatever situation the Lord has assigned to them, just as God has called them.
1 CORINTHIANS 7:17 NIV

Dear God, You called me away from an aimless, dark, and destructive journey to the life of a believing Christ follower. Help me live like I am, in fact, a Christ follower in the circumstances You send my way. You called. I answered. Help me remember You invited me to this journey and I agreed to walk with You. May I never forget You are my traveling companion. I don't want to get ahead of You. I also don't want to fall behind. Amen.

What I Have

Whoever keeps his word, in him truly the love of God is perfected. By this we may know that we are in him.
1 John 2:5 esv

Dear God, my purpose in life is not to become a spiritual spectator. You want me to read Your Word and obey Your commands. When I do, I accept Your love and share it. People notice the difference, and they want to know what I have that they don't. They will want to know where to find it. When I understand You want me to share Your rescue plan, then I shouldn't be surprised when I see people rescued. Amen.

Keep Me from Sounding Spiritual

Concentrate on doing your best for God, work you won't be ashamed of, laying out the truth plain and simple. Stay clear of pious talk that is only talk. Words are not mere words, you know.
2 Timothy 2:15–16 msg

Dear God, let my work be an expression of my purpose— the one You created for me. May a good work ethic extend to my understanding of You and what You want for me. When I become better acquainted with Your ways I can more clearly share Your truth, Your way, Your life. Keep me from sounding spiritual. Make me a man after Your own heart. Amen.

How Good You Are

*You are a chosen people. You are royal priests, a holy
nation, God's very own possession. As a result, you
can show others the goodness of God, for he called
you out of the darkness into his wonderful light.*
1 PETER 2:9 NLT

Dear God, You want to set me apart so I can do something for You that You created me to do. When I met You,
it was like living my entire life deep in a cave and having
an invitation to step into noontime sunshine for the very
first time. Help me call out to those still living in spiritual
darkness. They need to know how brilliant You are. Amen.

The Purpose of Friendships

*I'm a friend and companion of all who fear you,
of those committed to living by your rules.*
PSALM 119:63 MSG

Dear God, Your purpose for my life includes plans,
provision, and perspective. If I really want Your purpose
for my life, then I will need to be careful that my
friendships include people who encourage me to fulfill
my purpose. If I want Your best, I will guard my heart
from those who make fun of You. May I seek Your
guidance in making friends. May the love You
want me to share extend to all. Amen.

My Friends

The Power of Dependability

God created the absolute need for relationship. When relationships are scarce, you feel oppressive loneliness. This can be true even if you are in the company of other people. How is this possible? How can you be surrounded by people and still feel alone? Isn't it enough to share space with other humans?

Think of it this way: if you place multiple electric appliances in the same room but never connect them to a power source, they can't function like they are supposed to. Humans react in a similar way. You can share space with others but never allow yourself to connect in a meaningful way. When you refuse to engage people with mutual transparency, the result is surface relationships and faulty connections. Small talk, sports scores, and talking about what you do for a living will never get you to a place of real friendship. This may be why most people settle for a long list of acquaintances but never really think of them as friends. Is it possible that people explore your social media profile but never really know you?

Your most important relationship and friendship is with God. Don't treat Him like an acquaintance. He insists on transparency. He wants you to share the good, the bad, and everything you'd rather hide. You can't keep anything secret from God, so stop trying. He can help you, but you never help yourself by either refusing to be honest when you talk to God or deciding you just can't talk to Him anymore. Deuteronomy 7:9 (NLT) says, "He is the faithful God who keeps his covenant for a thousand generations and lavishes his unfailing love on those who love him and obey his commands."

The second most important relationship is the one you have with your wife. She was created to be your companion. She should be the closest human relationship you will ever experience. Genesis 2:24 (NKJV) says, "A man shall leave his father and mother and be joined to his wife." She will be the one who witnesses your greatest joys and deepest regrets.

The natural progression of relationships moves on to your children and extended family. You need them. They need you. Sometimes these relationships can seem greater than the bond between husband and wife, but they aren't meant to be.

Filtering further in God's relationship portfolio, you'll discover your church family followed by all other friends and coworkers. The greatest reason for this trip around the relational cul-de-sac is that God designed you for friendship.

Perhaps the greatest practical application for relationships is that when you develop relationships, it helps you identify those you can depend on and those who can depend on you. God created you to be interdependent. Acts 20:34–35 (MSG) says, "I have demonstrated to you how necessary it is to work on behalf of the weak and not exploit them. You'll not likely go wrong here if you keep remembering that our Master said, 'You're far happier giving than getting.'"

Some people seek friendships based on what the other person can do for them, but God says we should seek out people who need help and then, offer help. If you can accept this idea, it will mean you invest in others with no expectation of return. You might experience surprise when they show up to help in your time of need. This can be true of your wife, children, family, church family, and every other friend you will ever have.

Proverbs 18:24 (NKJV) says, "A man who has friends must himself be friendly." The truth is friends come and go, but real friends are discovered in the relational currency of your willingness to be friendly. Jesus showed us what it's like to love people who may never love in return, but it never stopped Him from loving. On the other hand, He had friends who were close to Him who depended on Him, and while they all experienced moments of failure, eleven of them were as dependable as humans can be who choose to accept God's help.

Yes, choose your friends wisely. Yes, your closest friends will be those who encourage your faith. Yes, start with God, your wife, and immediate family. Branch out to those who can give you nothing in return. Let the dependability of relationship start with you. Realize not all friendships are forever. Your best relationships can follow you into eternity.

Got it? Go. Be a friend.

Relationship's Source

My beloved friends, let us continue to love each other
since love comes from God. Everyone who loves is born
of God and experiences a relationship with God. The
person who refuses to love doesn't know the first thing
about God, because God is love—so you can't know him
if you don't love. This is how God showed his love for us:
God sent his only Son into the world so we might live
through him. This is the kind of love we are talking about—
not that we once upon a time loved God, but that he loved
us and sent his Son as a sacrifice to clear away our sins and
the damage they've done to our relationship with God.
1 JOHN 4:7–10 MSG

―――――――――――――――

Braided Rope Friendships

By yourself you're unprotected. With a friend you
can face the worst. Can you round up a third?
A three-stranded rope isn't easily snapped.
ECCLESIASTES 4:12 MSG

Dear God, good friends keep me honest and
compassionate, and they encourage Your purpose
in me. When I insist on walking alone I can get into
trouble. Help me face the worst by depending on the
friends You bring to me and the mercy You offer. Amen.

Inconvenient Love

"Greater love has no one than this,
than to lay down one's life for his friends."
JOHN 15:13 NKJV

Dear God, Your Son showed me what the ultimate
in friendships looks like. He knew I would need to be
rescued from my own sin-filled past, and He gave everything He had to make things right between me and You.
Let me remember the kind of love You give and learn to
love others even when it's not convenient. Amen.

False Expectations

Friends love through all kinds of weather,
and families stick together in all kinds of trouble.
PROVERBS 17:17 MSG

Dear God, friendships can be based on false expectations.
Some may want to be friends with me until they see me
struggle. In awkwardness they back away and find reasons
to stay away. I can do the same thing. Blue sky and sunny
day friendships are pleasant and rarely require much
investment. When I see brokenness in those I call friends,
help me lend a hand, spend some time, and weep with
those who weep during gray skies and dark nights. Amen.

Further Away from Your Voice

Do not be deceived:
"Bad company ruins good morals."
1 CORINTHIANS 15:33 ESV

Dear God, I can't believe how easy it is to find
people who don't really care about my faith, future,
and purpose. Allow me to be a friend to them without
falling victim to life choices that move me further
away from Your voice. Help me be a friend of sinners
who happens to first be a friend of Yours. Amen.

Recognize the Difference

The pleasantness of a friend springs
from their heartfelt advice.
PROVERBS 27:9 NIV

Dear God, when I accept advice from a friend, may I
recognize the way the advice matches the words I read
in the Bible. May my friends resist personal opinion and
follow Your life instructions. Help me recognize the
difference between advice that reflects the fruit of the
Spirit and advice that stinks of selfishness, revenge,
or untruth. Bring me pleasant friends. Amen.

More Important Than Fitting In

A man of many companions may come to ruin,
but there is a friend who sticks closer than a brother.
PROVERBS 18:24 ESV

Dear God, there is danger in mob friendships. With many
friends I can fall victim to peer pressure and find myself
agreeing with things I don't really believe, doing things
I never thought I would do, and saying things I regret.
Help me remember that in those moments my friendship
with You is more important than fitting in. Amen.

Limiting God?

Anyone who chooses to be a friend of
the world becomes an enemy of God.
JAMES 4:4 NIV

Dear God, help me remember that my friendships
with those who don't know You are meant to be an
introduction to You. When I set aside Your agenda in
favor of enjoying the lifestyle of those who don't follow
You, I diminish my reputation, limit Your impact,
and use my actions as a statement that You don't really
change people for the better. When I act like You
don't matter, people will believe me. Amen.

Confessing Other People's Sins

*A gossip goes around telling secrets, but those
who are trustworthy can keep a confidence.*
PROVERBS 11:13 NLT

Dear God, gossip is confessing other people's sins. Even
worse, gossip shares the worst about other humans
without even being sure it's true. A gossip shares without
permission. The information is passed on with a secret
happiness because I feel superior in sharing their bad
news. When someone shares something personal with me,
help me keep the information to myself. If I have to share
it with someone, let that someone be You. Amen.

A Path Hard Chosen

Do two walk together unless they have agreed to do so?
AMOS 3:3 NIV

Dear God, when I have a friend who decides to move
a direction I am uncomfortable with, help me determine
whether I can walk with that friend. Sometimes the
choices of people I care about mean I can't follow where
they go. There is a great sense of companionship when two
people in Your family walk the same way. You call that
unity. It's hard to walk with friends I believe are walking
toward danger. Help me pray for them and remind them
where they can find me when they choose to retreat
from their personal danger zone. Amen.

A "Count On" Kinda Friend

*Love each other with genuine affection,
and take delight in honoring each other.*
ROMANS 12:10 NLT

Dear God, I want to love others the way You love me.
May the choice to look out for the best interest of
others bring a depth to my relationships that convinces
me that I can count on my friends and they can count
on me. Help me honor others in the way I treat them
and things I say to and about them. Amen.

May I Introduce You to a Friend?

*When a man's ways please the LORD, he makes
even his enemies to be at peace with him.*
PROVERBS 16:7 NKJV

Dear God, when it comes to relationships You set
the bar. When I follow Your commands, the attributes
You want for Your family show up in the way I treat
people and the way I conduct myself. Your attributes
are pleasing to people who don't think they need You.
May my decisions please You and open the door
to introducing You to new friends. Amen.

My Extended Family

The Power of Legacy

You might be a son, father, brother, cousin, nephew, and grandson. You have family connections that place you squarely in the path of people who, for good or bad, influenced you. Depending on your family history, you either seek to break generational sin or you hold your family's spiritual legacy as a positive benchmark.

No matter how horrible you may feel your family has been, there is not a single person God cannot redeem. No matter how good your family may have been, there are still parts that were not perfect because perfection is unknown to mankind. You may be asking, "If there are faults in every family foundation, then why is extended family important?" God set things straight in Exodus 20:12 (NLT): "Honor your father and mother."

What does this kind of honor mean? It means to weigh the needs and opinions of your parents more highly than others. It means to respect them more deeply and esteem them above others. It does *not* mean that your relationship with your parents is the same in adulthood as it was when you were a child. Becoming an adult redefines the relationship, but it never ends it.

When God says you are to honor your father and mother, He doesn't provide loopholes or clauses. He does not say to honor them only if they deserve it or just when you feel like it. There is no legal language that sets out what constitutes a breach of contract between you and your parents. Parents are given commands as to how they raise and treat their children. Children are given commands as to how they treat their parents. Neither are contingent on the other. Even when parents have failed to follow God's parenting rules, He still expects children to honor their parents.

If you feel like God is asking too much, consider 1 Peter 4:8 (NLT): "Show deep love for each other, for love covers a multitude of sins." Many people have negative memories of their family. There may be a point where your parents made promises they were unable to keep, said things that hurt your feelings, or used untrue words that colored the way you thought of yourself. To honor someone who would do something like that seems counter to the way you want to treat your own children. Yet, God asks you to show deep love. He even commands you to pray for those who have hurt you (see Matthew 5:44).

The idea behind the phrase "love covers a multitude of sins" isn't about you paying for your sins or the sins of another by showing love. It means that when you love others, it's like throwing a blanket over their sins and protecting them from any gossip you could share about them. It extends the same forgiveness you received from God and demonstrates that the God who completely forgives can change those who follow Him.

Jesus says in John 13:34–35 (MSG), "Let me give you a new command: Love one another. In the same way I loved you, you love one another. This is how everyone will recognize that you are my disciples—when they see the love you have for each other."

Sometimes the only justification for forgiveness you can find is because God's Word says the love that shows forgiveness is what His family is supposed to offer. God sets the example, and this issue is no exception. He forgave you when you could offer nothing but poor decision-making. He loved you when "rebellious" was your middle name.

When your children see you honor your parents, it provides a very visible reason for your children to honor you as they move into adulthood. The idea of modeling extends far beyond the typical lessons of sharing, respect, and kindness.

Viewing your extended family as worthy of honor and respect shows honor and respect to the God who created family. It builds bridges where there had been walls. It extends friendship to those who seemed like enemies. It proves that obedience to the God who commanded you to love can result in positive change.

The honor you extend becomes a legacy. This honor becomes something remembered by both your parents and children alike. God's perspective is evident in Proverbs 20:7 (NKJV): "The righteous man walks in his integrity; his children are blessed after him." If you want to bless your children, honor your parents.

Enough Wisdom

*There will be terrible times in the last days. People will be
lovers of themselves, lovers of money, boastful, proud, abusive,
disobedient to their parents, ungrateful, unholy, without love,
unforgiving, slanderous, without self-control, brutal, not lovers
of the good, treacherous, rash, conceited, lovers of pleasure
rather than lovers of God—having a form of godliness but
denying its power. Have nothing to do with such people.*
2 TIMOTHY 3:1–5 NIV

Dear God, it's easy to think that I am only responsible
for myself and my immediate family. The verses I just
read indicate I am to be obedient to my parents. Even if
I believe this is talking about the time I spent at home as
a child, the verse also talks about the need to be grateful,
loving, and self-controlled. Even if I look at the verses in
this way, there is enough wisdom to bring me to a
place of honor toward my parents. Amen.

Honor Expressed

*A wise son makes a glad father,
but a foolish man despises his mother.*
PROVERBS 15:20 ESV

Dear God, I can spend time looking at lists of promises
broken, unkind words, and slights I recall from the
years I spent with my dad, mom, or both. I can convince
myself that my honor and kindness are undeserved
and should be withheld. Help me show wisdom by
honoring the ones who gave me life. Amen.

Stories Shared

Listen to your father, who gave you life,
and do not despise your mother when she is old.
PROVERBS 23:22 NIV

Dear God, when I don't understand why my parents
made the choices they made, help me spend time
getting to know them as an adult. Help me want to hear
their stories and help them when I can. In doing so,
help me become a friend who is also a son. I know my
relationship with my parents changes as an adult, so may
I also help understand their difficulties and how to
lend a hand without stealing their dignity. Amen.

Right and Humble

In the same way, you who are younger must accept
the authority of the elders. And all of you, dress
yourselves in humility as you relate to one another,
for "God opposes the proud but gives grace to the humble."
1 PETER 5:5 NLT

Dear God, stop me from thinking I know more
than my parents. Keep the idea of old school from my
thinking. It is true I will differ in my actions and reactions
than my parents, but You say I can still learn from their
life story. You would rather I be right and humble than
wrong and proud. May I forgive because I need to and
love because it leaves me without regret. Amen.

Bless—In God's Name

If a widow has family members to take care of her,
let them learn that religion begins at their own doorstep
and that they should pay back with gratitude some of
what they have received. This pleases God immensely.
1 TIMOTHY 5:4 MSG

Dear God, help me take inventory of my extended family
and see if there is someone I can bless in Your name.
May my actions be in keeping with Your love for me.
May those same actions be a blessing, comfort,
and help to family members who might never have
suspected how You would send help. Amen.

As I Trust

Give to everyone what you owe them: If you
owe taxes, pay taxes; if revenue, then revenue;
if respect, then respect; if honor, then honor.
ROMANS 13:7 NIV

Dear God, if I owe taxes, You want me to pay it. If I
need to pay a bill, then You want me to pay it, and if I
owe honor, then I should honor. You tell me I am to
honor my parents. Help me remember that in Your eyes
this obligation is no different than the need to pay taxes
or bills. I should honor them because You asked.
As I trust in You help me obey. Amen.

Don't Make That Kind of Decision

As they did not like to retain God in their knowledge,
God gave them over to a debased mind, to do those things
which are not fitting; being filled with all unrighteousness,
sexual immorality, wickedness, covetousness, maliciousness;
full of envy, murder, strife, deceit, evil-mindedness; they are
whisperers, backbiters, haters of God, violent, proud, boasters,
inventors of evil things, disobedient to parents.
ROMANS 1:28–30 NKJV

Dear God, I don't want to be one of those people
who has made the decision to remove You from the
position of God. While my opinion will never change
who You are, it does mean I could more easily decide
I can do what I want because I believe You are not
important enough to give me instructions worth
following. When I refuse to honor my parents, I am
making that kind of decision. Stop me. Amen.

Fence Mending

I want you to get out there and walk—better yet, run!—
on the road God called you to travel. I don't want any of you
sitting around on your hands. I don't want anyone strolling
off, down some path that goes nowhere. And mark that you do
this with humility and discipline—not in fits and starts, but
steadily, pouring yourselves out for each other in acts of love,
alert at noticing differences and quick at mending fences.
EPHESIANS 4:2–3 MSG

The Golden Rule

"Here is a simple, rule-of-thumb guide for behavior:
Ask yourself what you want people to do for you,
then grab the initiative and do it for them."
MATTHEW 7:12 MSG

Dear God, if everyone did what Your rule-of-thumb guide
commands, then there would never be conflict, but not
everyone will follow this rule. The primary person I am
responsible for is myself. I can't make my extended family
treat me the way I want to be treated, but I can treat them
in honorable ways. That may come as a surprise to them,
but it is living life the way You say it should be lived. Amen.

Already on the Job

Unless the LORD builds the house, those who
build it labor in vain. Unless the LORD watches
over the city, the watchman stays awake in vain.
PSALM 127:1 ESV

Dear God, when I am certain I cannot honor my
parents, when I am uncomfortable offering peace
when I was offered only pain, and when I think that
perhaps this command only applies to others, help me
remember that Your words were not for the few, but for
all of mankind. Remind me that I am not alone.
You build my house into a home. You secure my life.
When I work to protect what You've given me,
remind me You are already on the job. Amen.

My Nation

The Power of Community

Community starts with an individual, expands to families, groups into neighborhoods, organizes as cities existing within geographical areas, and when combined make a nation. Community isn't just allegiance to a country, voting in a state election, or attending a county fair. Community is—people.

There are bake sales, pancake feeds, and school fund-raisers. There are school trips, learning opportunities, and national monuments. There are long-distance relatives, friends who've moved away, and people you've yet to meet. There are mountains, valleys, and rivers to enjoy. But when you remove all the places and opportunities, you are left with *people*.

These individuals share in your work, identify with your struggle, and are companions when you're lonely. These people will often work toward the common good in their zip code. They care about their region. They invest in the future of their country.

Philippians 2:1–4 (MSG) says, "If you've gotten anything at all out of following Christ, if his love has made any difference in your life, if being in a community of the Spirit means anything to you, if you have a heart, if you care—then do me a favor: Agree with each other, love each other, be deep-spirited friends. Don't push your way to the front; don't sweet-talk your way to the top. Put yourself aside, and help others get ahead. Don't be obsessed with getting your own advantage. Forget yourselves long enough to lend a helping hand."

The sense of community you learn by being involved with other Christ followers should contribute to the way you view your national community. When you identify with God's purpose, you have the opportunity "to do what is right, to love mercy, and to walk humbly with your God" (Micah 6:8 NLT).

This modeled behavior impacts your community and ripples to all edges of your country, shines a light on all that's better, and challenges your children to follow your lead.

Wes was one of those models. He routinely visited the offices of a variety of organizations writing checks to help fund projects that made life better for those in his community. He never talked about it. Most people had no idea until Wes passed away. It was only then that those organizations felt the freedom to share the story of Wes's generosity. Not every organization Wes helped was a ministry, but this just gave Wes the opportunity to make sure they knew the motivation for the gift. Those conversations had a different impact.

Wes understood the value of community. He understood that as one who followed Christ, he was also supposed to help those in this *common* community. More than that, Wes knew that there was a deep purpose behind using what God had given to affect people who needed to know the God who rescues. Perhaps Wes remembered 1 John 2:15–17 (MSG), which says, "Don't love the world's ways. Don't love the world's goods. Love of the world squeezes out love for the Father. Practically everything that goes on in the world—wanting your own way, wanting everything for yourself, wanting to appear important—has nothing to do with the Father. It just isolates you from him. The world and all its wanting, wanting, wanting is on the way out—but whoever does what God wants is set for eternity."

In this moment you can't possess what you own in eternity. It's yours—you just can't have it yet. Your temporary home here is like living in a tent when a mansion is waiting for your future arrival. But if you had to choose between the two, would you prefer the tent? Wes invested in the future because the people he helped were people he wanted to see again when God asked him to invest his last gift. If Wes had been a "tent enthusiast," he would have invested in gold-plated tent poles and refused his community investments. Instead, he chose to believe the tent was temporary housing.

Hebrews 13:16 (ESV) says, "Do not neglect to do good and to share what you have, for such sacrifices are pleasing to God." Did you know that if it weren't for Christians seeking the common good of all people, there would be no hospitals? Did you know that universities were the gift of Christians who believed all people should have access to education? In times of need—Christians step up.

Marvelously Functioning

*We are like the various parts of a human body. Each part
gets its meaning from the body as a whole, not the other
way around. The body we're talking about is Christ's body
of chosen people. Each of us finds our meaning and function
as a part of his body. But as a chopped-off finger or cut-off
toe we wouldn't amount to much, would we? So since we find
ourselves fashioned into all these excellently formed and
marvelously functioning parts in Christ's body, let's just go
ahead and be what we were made to be, without enviously
or pridefully comparing ourselves with each other,
or trying to be something we aren't.*
ROMANS 12:4–6 MSG

True for Me

*God said, "It is not good for the man to be alone.
I will make a helper who is just right for him."*
GENESIS 2:18 NLT

Dear God, from the beginning You recognized that
mankind would need the companionship of our own
kind. More than a pet dog. More than a horse to ride.
More than a cat to care for. We needed others to help
us. This is true for marriage and family. This is true
for cities and nations. It is true for me. Amen.

Not about Me

Behold, how good and pleasant it
is when brothers dwell in unity!
PSALM 133:1 ESV

Dear God, You tell me it is best to be patient when others
are not at the same place in their journey as I am. They
may be behind me or further ahead. They need to be
patient with me too. When we understand we can't be at
the exact same place at the exact same time, then unity
becomes possible because we rally around the object of our
rescue rather than the condition of the rescued. Thanks
for the reminder that this life is not about me. Amen.

You Asked Me to Help

Do not forget to show hospitality to strangers.
HEBREWS 13:2 NIV

Dear God, I understand the idea of helping family,
and I try to help my neighbors, but showing hospitality
to people I don't even know sounds like You're asking
me to go above and beyond. You are. You want Your
family to be known for stepping outside their comfort
zone, stepping up when help is needed, and stepping
back to give You glory. Help me do what You ask, not
because I want to be recognized, but because You asked
me to help and You taught me to love. Amen.

Burdens Shared

Share each other's burdens,
and in this way obey the law of Christ.
GALATIANS 6:2 NLT

Dear God, if I try to carry a piece of furniture by myself I
might be able to move it to its new location, but if I have
help I can move it much faster and with less difficulty.
This is true with my Christian family. When I share the
burdens of others, they struggle less. When others join
me in my struggle, I am encouraged and discover comfort.
This is what You ask. Help me do what You ask. Amen.

Answer Their Prayers

"Give to the one who asks you, and do not turn
away from the one who wants to borrow from you."
MATTHEW 5:42 NIV

Dear God, You have given me everything. Help me give
when others ask me for help. May I offer what I have as
Your gift to the one in need. You take care of me, and You
ask me to use Your gifts to help others—who may not
even realize You're answering their prayers. Amen.

My Response to Others

Let nothing be done through selfish ambition or conceit, but in lowliness of mind let each esteem others better than himself.
PHILIPPIANS 2:3 NKJV

Dear God, sometimes the actions of others make it hard to think of them as better. When I observe bad behavior it is difficult to want to treat them with even a hint of honor. Maybe the reason You want me to do this is because in some ways You've done this for me. You treated me as someone You cherished when I thought You were a joke. If You can treat me with such incredible love, help me use Your example to improve my response to others. Amen.

Help However I Can

Let each of you look not only to his own interests, but also to the interests of others.
PHILIPPIANS 2:4 ESV

Dear God, I have dreams. I have plans. I want to experience success. The things I am interested in are important to me. You want me to be interested in the dreams of others. You want me to help however I can. Cause me to remember that relationship is my connection to You, and to people You created with their own dreams and plans. Amen.

The Way to Live

The first thing I want you to do is pray. Pray every way you know how, for everyone you know. Pray especially for rulers and their governments to rule well so we can be quietly about our business of living simply, in humble contemplation. This is the way our Savior God wants us to live.
1 TIMOTHY 2:1–3 MSG

Dear God, there is power in prayer because when
I pray I am talking to the One who is all-powerful.
May the content of my prayers honor You and
remember the needs of those I care about and
the leaders who need Your help. Amen.

The Need to Hear

"You will be my witnesses, telling people about me everywhere—in Jerusalem, throughout Judea, in Samaria, and to the ends of the earth."
ACTS 1:8 NLT

Dear God, I am a witness. I have observed Your
goodness, and You want me to tell others so they have
an opportunity to witness what I have seen, heard,
and believe. You are good, and there is no one in the
world who does not need to hear about You. Amen.

My Dreams

The Power of a Heart's Desire

Someone reading these words had a dream of being a professional athlete. Someone wanted to start a business. Someone wanted to fund a well in a faraway country so people who live there could drink clean water.

Jack was that last kind of dreamer. He started by rounding up thousands of pairs of shoes and boots and filled shipping containers with a specific African destination. He worked with a small Christian college in Tanzania, especially with its founder, Eludi. Together these men made sure the shoes found new feet. Eludi would come to the United States, and Jack would make sure his friend had plenty of places where he could share his dream.

Jack wasn't sure if he could ever be a traditional missionary, but he had a bigger dream. It started with shoes and escalated to helping Eludi find support from Christians in middle America. The small Tanzanian college grew to include a medical center.

With Eludi well stocked with shoes and medical supplies, Jack turned his attention to another way to help his friend. Jack's dream expanded to clean drinking water. Jack had the know-how, and Eludi had a know-God need. Jack prayed. God gave him the desire of his heart. Equipment was acquired, and an aging American cowboy led the work at that small Christian college in Tanzania—the same

Christian college that had started as Eludi's dream. People came from miles around to the campus to get free clean water. Eludi shared the love of Jesus. People came to know Jesus, the source of living water. Two more wells were dug. More people came.

Different men from different continents with different backgrounds used their God-blessed skills as a platform for something big. Both men could give the same advice as King David who wrote in Psalm 37:4 (NIV), "Take delight in the LORD, and he will give you the desires of your heart."

God did not promise that you could ask for all the wealth in the world, or all the fame in Hollywood, or the notoriety of a king, and that He would answer these prayers spoken in selfishness. David, who was a king, knew that the desires of men's hearts are worthless if men don't first "take delight in the LORD." The desires of your heart change when God comes first. Jack's dream began and ended with God. Eludi's dream followed a similar path. God brought two dreamers together, and lives were changed because they sought God first (see Matthew 6:33).

The power of a heart's desire is the blending of your purpose with God's plan. The closer you are to God, the more possible it becomes to take a God-inspired dream and watch it move from impossible to reality. God never asked you to make a wish list of everything that would make your life easier, provide you with greater income, or make people think more highly of you.

In fact, God promised trouble (see 1 Peter 2:21). He also said that money was the least of your worries because He would meet your needs (see Philippians 4:19). Proverbs 11:2 (ESV) places a little polish on the subject of arrogance, saying, "When pride comes, then comes disgrace, but with the humble is wisdom."

God seems delighted when His people praise His greatness and then dream big. Nehemiah's big dream was rebuilding the wall of Jerusalem. Solomon dreamed of building God's temple. Zacchaeus dreamed of meeting Jesus. God gave them the desires of their heart. What's your close-to-God's-heart dream?

If you want another perspective on what it looks like to "take delight in the Lord," consider 1 John 2:3–6 (MSG): "Here's how we can be sure that we know God in the right way: Keep his commandments. If someone claims, 'I know him well!' but doesn't keep his commandments, he's obviously a liar. His life doesn't match his words. But the one who keeps God's word is the person in whom we see God's mature love. This is the only way to be sure we're in God. Anyone who claims to be intimate with God ought to live the same kind of life Jesus lived."

The relationship between God and mankind is key to understanding how God's provision and your dream should connect to meet needs, develop stories of His faithfulness, and place you squarely on the path of God's will.

Small Faith—Big Move

"You don't have enough faith," Jesus told them. "I tell you the truth, if you had faith even as small as a mustard seed, you could say to this mountain, 'Move from here to there,' and it would move. Nothing would be impossible."
MATTHEW 17:20 NLT

Accomplish

I can do all things through
Christ who strengthens me.
PHILIPPIANS 4:13 NKJV

Dear God, when You give me strength, I can accomplish everything You want for me. If You don't strengthen me, I will struggle and I will fail because my dream will end in something You know is not good for me. Help me dream in a way that allows me access to Your strength. Help me succeed in the way You want for me. Amen.

Keep Me Company

"Don't panic. I'm with you. There's no need to fear
for I'm your God. I'll give you strength. I'll help you.
I'll hold you steady, keep a firm grip on you."
ISAIAH 41:10 MSG

Dear God, when I fear the unknown, when my
heart melts because of the size of my dream, and when
others tell me it can't be done, remind me that my
strength comes from You and not my personal resolve.
Like a good parent, watch over me and point me in a
better direction. Keep me steady. Keep me company.
Keep me following You. Amen.

Dreams Abandoned

God is my helper. The Lord keeps me alive!
PSALM 54:4 NLT

Dear God, You help me. You keep me alive. It can
be easy to think that You are lucky to have certain
people on Your team. But if You do the helping and
the keeping, what more can anyone add except to be
helped and to accept the life You offer? My dreams
can't exist apart from what You do to help. If You
think my dream needs adjustment, please help me
abandon my dream in favor of Your help. Amen.

God's Way of Thinking

If God is for us, who can be against us?
ROMANS 8:31 NIV

Dear God, I don't ever want to believe that each plan I make is rubber-stamped with Your blessing. You don't say that *because* You are for me, no one can be against me. You say *if* You are for me. This means that my priorities need to match Yours. In the end, when I come around to Your way of thinking, dreams come to life. Amen.

Reaches to My Dreams

"Behold, I am the LORD, the God of all flesh. Is anything too hard for me?"
JEREMIAH 32:27 ESV

Dear God, I want to rely on You. Remind me that no one would exist without You. I need to be reminded that nothing would hold together if You didn't take this responsibility as the God of the universe. Nothing is too hard for You. This truth reaches all the way to my greatest dreams, most complete plans, and the way I choose to include You in my everyday life. Amen.

Think. Correctly.

Commit your works to the LORD,
and your thoughts will be established.
PROVERBS 16:3 NKJV

Dear God, help me remember that You did not say
You will help me do anything I set my mind to do.
You said that if I dedicate my work to You that You
will help me think correctly about that work. This
could mean You help me see I need to walk toward
my goal, or it could mean I have not been following
a productive goal. Sometimes you have a walk-away
plan. This is just the protection I need. Amen.

A World of Misinformation

My dear friends, don't believe everything you hear.
Carefully weigh and examine what people tell you.
Not everyone who talks about God comes from God.
1 JOHN 4:1 MSG

Dear God, I live in a world of misinformation.
It comes in the form of gossip and half-truths, and it
can arrive on the lips of those I consider trustworthy.
When humans share with humans, there will always be
misinformation. Help me compare what I hear with what
You say. If there is contradiction in their message, help me
reject it as I pursue Your dream for me. Amen.

Don't Waste Time

The word of God is alive and active. Sharper than any
double-edged sword, it penetrates even to dividing
soul and spirit, joints and marrow; it judges
the thoughts and attitudes of the heart.
HEBREWS 4:12 NIV

Dear God, when I am selfish, I see my true condition
when I read Your Word. If I am dishonest, rebellious,
and unforgiving, Your Word shines a spotlight on these
stumbling blocks. You don't want me to be unaware of
my true condition. I can ignore Your warnings and trip,
or I can tell You all about my human nature and ask
You to lead me around the things that slow me down.
I don't want to waste time. Amen.

The Invitation

God can do anything, you know—far more than you
could ever imagine or guess or request in your wildest
dreams! He does it not by pushing us around but by
working within us, his Spirit deeply and gently within us.
EPHESIANS 3:20 MSG

Dear God, You are not a bully that I should fear to follow.
You are not a dictator that I have to follow. You are a
friend who invites me to join You on a journey to a place
I didn't know I wanted to be. You work inside me to
encourage me to trust, to follow, and to obey. Amen.

His Better Direction

There are many plans in a man's heart,
nevertheless the LORD's counsel—that will stand.
PROVERBS 19:21 NKJV

Dear God, I have dreams. There are things I plan to
do, but I don't know the obstacles ahead, I don't know
the things hidden from view, and I wouldn't even know
the right steps to take if it weren't for Your guidance.
Help me be willing to stop following my plan when
You guide in a better direction. Amen.

Where You Want Me to Move

"I prayed to GOD, 'Dear GOD, my Master, you created earth
and sky by your great power—by merely stretching
out your arm! There is nothing you can't do.'"
JEREMIAH 32:17 MSG

Dear God, I want this prayer to mirror Jeremiah's. You
created everything, and You can do anything. If You are
for me, then I can move to where You want me to move
and You will make sure I get there. You are the Maker
of the earth and sky, and when it comes to my future the
only one who can stop Your plans for me—is me. Help
me never get in the way of Your good plan. Amen.

My Fulfillment

The Power of Contentment

If there were two words that could be a close replacement for the word *contentment*, those words might be *fulfillment* and *satisfaction*. Too often the word you might associate with contentment, however, is the word *settling*.

Keep reading to understand why contentment never settles. Hebrews 13:5 (ESV) says, "Keep your life free from love of money, and be content with what you have." You might assume God is asking you to settle for less income, to get by the best you can, or to accept less resources than you want. These conclusions invite discontent. Maybe that's why the rest of the verse explains why contentment is much more than settling for something you don't really like: "For he has said, 'I will never leave you nor forsake you.'"

God is asking you to discover satisfaction and fulfillment, not by pursuing money, but trusting God's promise to always be with you. There is more satisfaction in a God relationship than in anything you can purchase.

Earlier you read that joy is associated with contentment. Satisfaction supplies the resource of peace. Psalm 145:16 (NLT) says of God, "When you open your hand, you satisfy the hunger and thirst of every living thing." Imagine the anxiety removal that occurs when you realize that God loves and takes care of you. Would you pass up God's care and companionship for money? Isaiah 31:1 (ESV) speaks to this trade of fools: "Woe to those who go down to Egypt for help and rely on horses, who trust in chariots because they are many and in horsemen because they are very strong, but do not look to the Holy One of Israel or consult the Lord!"

How would it change your contentment perspective to remember that satisfaction and peace are available *because* you have a friendship with God? To display the flip side of the contentment coin, God provides a pretty distasteful word picture of what discontentment looks like. Proverbs 30:15 (msg) says, "A leech has twin daughters named 'Gimme' and 'Gimme more.'" Discontentment is a leech. Never fulfilled—never satisfied.

Leeches live off the lifeblood of others. They take what's not theirs, and they're always hungry for more. This isn't a question of personal initiative, but a bloodthirsty pursuit of instant gratification at any cost. Maybe that's why God has told us not to worry about what we eat or what we wear (see Matthew 6:25–29). He takes care of it.

If you have dreams, follow them. If you have goals, work to achieve them. If you have plans, ask God for help and input. Then when God has something else in mind you can be satisfied knowing you were not complacent (unwilling to change), but content (satisfied that God's response is trustworthy).

If you wonder whether being discontent is actually harmful, you should know that being discontent with what you have (or don't have) leads to envy, jealousy, and covetousness. Being discontent may mean you are at war with God (see Acts 5:39). Being discontent with God's provision may lead to anger, mistrust, and disrespect. A prime example of this was the forty years the Israelites wandered in the wilderness.

Contentment agrees with God's good plans. Contentment appreciates God's provisions. Contentment values God's friendship. On the other hand, discontentment is the belief that God's plans are flawed, His provisions are lacking, and friendship with Him means diminished freedom.

You experience satisfaction when you are content. Contentment recognizes the better plan of God. It surrenders the responsibility of calling the shots. It welcomes the adventure of whatever comes next.

Psalm 90:14 (NLT) says, "Satisfy us each morning with your unfailing love, so we may sing for joy to the end of our lives." If the psalmist was asking God to satisfy (deliver contentment), then you can believe that contentment is a gift God is willing to give—when you're willing to ask. It will require a change in thinking, in responding, and in trusting. Contentment is a personal choice requiring you to take action on what you believe to be true about God. If He is more than enough, then contentment should follow that conclusion. If you feel God is lacking, then you will resist contentment while trying to meet your own needs.

Your children can avoid wasting time when they learn from you that chasing stuff is never time well spent. Chasing God is the only race you're guaranteed to win—every time.

Richly Content

Oh, bless our God, you peoples! And make the voice of His praise to be heard, who keeps our soul among the living, and does not allow our feet to be moved. For You, O God, have tested us; You have refined us as silver is refined. You brought us into the net; You laid affliction on our backs. You have caused men to ride over our heads; we went through fire and through water; but You brought us out to rich fulfillment.
PSALM 66:8–12 NKJV

Lead On

Now you've got my feet on the life path, all radiant from the shining of your face. Ever since you took my hand, I'm on the right way.
PSALM 16:11 MSG

Dear God, it shouldn't surprise me that knowing where I'm going, understanding my purpose, and sharing the journey with You ends in contentment. I believe I should have a purpose, and I believe You have something for me to do. Take my hand, light my way, lead me on. I want to be completely satisfied in Your presence. Amen.

Desperately Seeking Satisfaction

Just as Death and Destruction are never satisfied,
so human desire is never satisfied.
PROVERBS 27:20 NLT

Dear God, it's human nature to resist contentment.
Death never ends, and destruction can become an
addiction. I can possess and want more. I can earn
and never feel I have enough. This is why it makes
sense for me to seek satisfaction in something that
can actually satisfy. Help me resist the lure of what
satisfies only for a limited time. Amen.

False Expectations

The one who loves money is never satisfied with money,
nor the one who loves wealth with big profits.
ECCLESIASTES 5:10 MSG

Dear God, why is it so easy to believe that money will
satisfy me? A little money doesn't seem to be enough,
and more than enough money soon becomes too little.
My expectations rise with every pay raise and bonus.
Money disappoints because everything I can buy with
money breaks, decays, and fails. If I buy something it
will need repair. All the bright shiny things I want
will one day populate a landfill. Help me find
contentment in a better direction. Amen.

Keep Your Focus

As for me, I will be vindicated and will see your face;
when I awake, I will be satisfied with seeing your likeness.
PSALM 17:15 NIV

Dear God, when I see the worst side of humanity,
when I am misjudged and criticized, and when I am
mistreated, help me focus on where contentment is
found—You. It is easy to watch how people treat each
other and invite discontent to a conversation. I need to
be reminded that You are just and judge correctly, You
treat me better than I will ever deserve, and You paid the
sin price for all humanity. Let me keep my eyes on
You—and discover contentment. Amen.

My Satisfaction

I will be fully satisfied as with the richest of foods;
with singing lips my mouth will praise you.
PSALM 63:5 NIV

Dear God, complete satisfaction leads me to share
where it came from. Being content urges me to praise
You for this wonderful gift. Contentment causes me
to become historical. Help me look back at my story
and remember the long line of good gifts from
Your hand. You are my satisfaction. Amen.

Welcome to the Authentic

The backslider in heart will be filled with his own ways, but a good man will be satisfied from above.
PROVERBS 14:14 NKJV

Dear God, when I drift from my place in Your presence I can cling only to false satisfaction, pretend contentment, and momentary fulfillment. I want to accept Your invitation to return to authentic satisfaction in a friendship with You, and not in an unhealthy relationship with what's-in-it-for-me circumstances. Amen.

═══════════════

Winning Scenario

But godliness with contentment is great gain.
1 TIMOTHY 6:6 NIV

Dear God, following You and being satisfied with You leads to a solid win for me. I don't have to settle for something that doesn't satisfy, but I can become settled deep within when I see the fulfillment of Your promises and follow Your rules. Amen.

Contentment: A Moving Target?

If we have bread on the table and
shoes on our feet, that's enough.
1 TIMOTHY 6:8 MSG

Dear God, it can become easy to think that if I could
own a certain car, buy a certain house, or wear certain
clothes, that I would be satisfied, but each step up in the
quality of "things" can plant new seeds of discontent.
Suddenly the new things I own are no longer the "right"
definition of contentment. When I accept the basics
from Your hand, help me recognize that contentment
can be found much sooner than I thought. Amen.

Becoming Transparent

Be content with who you are, and don't put on airs.
1 PETER 5:6 MSG

Dear God, it's hard to believe I am supposed to be satisfied
with who I am. No human knows more about me than I
do. I am not perfect, and I'm not always as transparent with
You and others as I should be. There are even times when
I am tempted to pretend I am more successful than I am.
Help me become comfortable in my own skin and choose
humility over going fishing for a compliment. Amen.

The Power of God's Forgiveness

When you're on a journey with Jesus it means that you're walking away from something and toward something else. It means turning your back on what led you away from your journey and focus on Jesus, "who both began and finished this race we're in. Study how he did it. Because he never lost sight of where he was headed—that exhilarating finish in and with God—he could put up with anything along the way: Cross, shame, whatever. And now he's there, in the place of honor, right alongside God. When you find yourselves flagging in your faith, go over that story again, item by item, that long litany of hostility he plowed through. That will shoot adrenaline into your souls!" (Hebrews 12:2–3 MSG).

Forgiveness is all about Jesus. You can't buy it because it's not for sale. You can't rent it because it must be new. You can't earn it because it's a gift. Forgiveness requires a sacrifice, and that sacrifice must be perfect. Because you need forgiveness it proves that imperfection exists within you (see Romans 3:10–12). Jesus was the only perfect sacrifice (see Hebrews 9:14). God accepted His death as payment for your sin (see Acts 17:30–31). God turned what should be punishment into a family reunion (see John 1:10–12).

Forgiveness is hard because it defies the logic of justice. If you are guilty you expect to be judged, found guilty, and rejected. When someone breaks a law against you it is common to want justice, to reject the offending party, and make sure they are well acquainted with their guilt. You might want them to pay for their sin, but your price can rise beyond anyone's ability to pay.

God's Son made it possible for sin to be forgiven. You can accept forgiveness. You don't have to be trapped in the sin of your past. You can be restored. Welcome to Good News Boulevard.

Your history was laid to rest so your future could share the stage with purpose, freedom, and hope. This is the power of forgiveness. It takes what shouldn't be possible and makes what's glorious attainable. It takes what seems off limits and offers the keys to God's kingdom. It takes the prodigal son and celebrates his homecoming. Beyond all this wonder God takes His forgiveness one step further. In Hebrews 8:12 (NLT), God says, "I will forgive their wickedness, and I will never again remember their sins."

God is the only One who can both forgive *and* forget. He never holds your past over you. He never tries to make you feel guilty. Romans 8:1–2 (MSG) says, "Those who enter into Christ's being-here-for-us no longer have to live under a continuous, low-lying black cloud. A new power is in operation. The Spirit of life in Christ, like a strong wind, has magnificently cleared the air, freeing you from a fated lifetime of brutal tyranny at the hands of sin and death."

Forgiveness removes eternal punishment and offers everything God has even though your sin should make you ineligible. This is a gift. It is free. It came at a terrible cost. Take it. Share the source. Forgive because you've been forgiven (see Ephesians 4:32).

It can seem like this gift is too good to be true, but

it's both good—and true. You could allow other people to convince you that absolute forgiveness is impossible. You could allow Satan to conduct daily seminars on why you are unforgivable. You could second-guess the meaning of forgiveness. And in trying to make up for your own sin, you cheapen the sacrifice Jesus offered to all humanity, including you.

If you refuse to trust that God has forgiven you, it's like taking the story of grace and saying you are the only one who can't be forgiven. Instead of combining your story of forgiveness with God's offer of mercy, you make the story about how bad you are instead of how good God is.

The story is never about your sin but about God's forgiveness. It's not about how much you've changed but who changed you. It's not about the quantity of sins but the quality of One who loved you enough to forgive. Accept forgiveness. Extend forgiveness.

Your past is a footnote. Your future is the book. Let God write your story. Let your children read that story today. Each day He's making you new.

Ignorance on Display

If we admit our sins—make a clean breast of them—he won't let us down; he'll be true to himself. He'll forgive our sins and purge us of all wrongdoing. If we claim that we've never sinned, we out-and-out contradict God—make a liar out of him. A claim like that only shows off our ignorance of God.
1 JOHN 1:9–10 MSG

Used to Being Judged

"God sent his Son into the world not to judge the world, but to save the world through him."
JOHN 3:17 NLT

Dear God, humanity is used to being judged. People will judge my sense of fashion, my home, my car, and my family. They will judge my actions. I will be labeled by the mistakes I've made and by the "God rules" I have broken. When Jesus came He was not on a mission to judge but to rescue those who knew they were guilty. Your forgiveness established trust where being withdrawn was the norm. Thanks for coming with forgiveness. Amen.

Stop Counting

*Then Peter came to Him and said, "Lord, how often
shall my brother sin against me, and I forgive him?
Up to seven times?" Jesus said to him, "I do not say to
you, up to seven times, but up to seventy times seven."*
MATTHEW 18:21–22 NKJV

Dear God, I am grateful that You forgive me. Sometimes
I'm like Peter and wonder if there is a limit to my own
responsibility to forgive. I can feel generous and give people
a pretty long leash, but I still want Your blessing to cut
them down to size when they stomp on my last nerve. Help
me remember You never count the second chances You give
me. You never stop forgiving. Your grace never ends. Why
should I place limits where You never have? Amen.

My Time with You

*And as far as sunrise is from sunset,
he has separated us from our sins.*
PSALM 103:12 MSG

Dear God, there are times I keep my sin close. Sadly, I
want to be reminded of my failings so I am comfortable
slipping back into old sin. Sometimes I want to remember
my sin so I can work harder and not repeat them. Yet You
say that You completely remove my sin from Your record.
If You don't see my old sin, then help me to let it go so I
can get on with enjoying my time with You. Amen.

God's Plan in Motion

"Love your enemies, do good to those who hate you."
LUKE 6:27 NKJV

Dear God, if I am honest I want to see justice. Those who hurt me or my family need to be penalized. There are times Your grace seems amazing to me, but too generous for those who hurt me. Yet You ask me to love them. You ask me to do good things for them. It feels like I'm just encouraging their bad behavior, but maybe You can use my obedience to get their attention, change their thinking, and help them see their need for the very thing that allows me to forgive. Maybe You have other reasons. Give me patience and help me put Your plan in motion. Amen.

Right Living, Yet Flawed

There is not a righteous man on earth who does good and never sins.
ECCLESIASTES 7:20 ESV

Dear God, I can think of the most godly men I have ever known and yet there are flaws. As committed as they are to right living, they have let people down—and they have let You down. If there is any comfort, it has to be that I am not alone in my failings. I am not alone in needing rescue. I am not alone in receiving mercy and accepting grace. Everyone I know needs You. Amen.

In My Place

*He was pierced for our transgressions, he was crushed
for our iniquities; the punishment that brought us
peace was on him, and by his wounds we are healed.*
ISAIAH 53:5 NIV

Dear God, You say the penalty for sin is death. This truth
means that every human on earth deserves nothing more
than death. Yet Your Son died in my place. His wounds
represented the cost of Your rescue plan. I can have peace
because Jesus was punished in my place. His death was the
seal of rescue. When He came back to life I was invited
into Your family. Your plan was perfect. Thank You. Amen.

Cleanse Me

*Wash me thoroughly from my iniquity,
and cleanse me from my sin. For I acknowledge
my transgressions, and my sin is always before me.*
PSALM 51:2–3 NKJV

Dear God, when the stench of my sin became more
than I could stand, I considered Your rescue plan.
When all I can see is my failings, You remind me
of Your perfection. This isn't because You want me
to compare my failings with Your perfection. I can
never compare myself favorably to You. I need to be
aware of my sins so I can admit them to You and
discover forgiveness. Wash me. Cleanse me. I was
wrong, and I recognize and admit it. Amen.

Release Sin's Pressure

I said, "I'll make a clean breast of my failures to GOD." Suddenly the pressure was gone—my guilt dissolved, my sin disappeared.
PSALM 32:5 MSG

Dear God, my sin is like an overinflated tire. The more I sin, the weaker my old tire becomes. It is stretched, the shape is wrong, and everyone notices. Help me be completely transparent in sharing my failures with You. Release sin's pressure on me. Help me remember guilt is only for the unforgiven. Get me back on track. When sin's pressure builds, let me come to You immediately because I don't want to wait to be forgiven. Amen.

Overdue Conversations

You, Lord, are forgiving and good, abounding in love to all who call to you.
PSALM 86:5 NIV

Dear God, You don't subject me to a lecture when I come to You, admitting I was wrong again. The fact that I come to You means I recognize my sin. You forgive. Your love is overwhelming. Your answers are good. You have just been waiting for me to call. Help me avoid extending overdue conversations with You. Amen.

My Future

The Power of Ultimate Hope

You might view life as something you're starting to live fully, or you might view it as the patriarch of a growing family. You might be someone who spends more time thinking about what comes next. If you are a Christ follower, never forget what Philippians 3:20 (MSG) says: "There's far more to life for us. We're citizens of high heaven! We're waiting the arrival of the Savior, the Master, Jesus Christ, who will transform our earthy bodies into glorious bodies like his own."

God had no beginning, and He makes sure your existence doesn't end. Your body is just temporary housing. Ecclesiastes 3:20 (ESV) says, "All are from the dust, and to dust all return." What you're left with at your end of life is the assurance of hope linked to the God who gave you a soul that cannot be reduced to dust. The assurance of hope in this transition from brokenness and trouble is that "there will be no more death or sorrow or crying or pain. All these things are gone forever" (Revelation 21:4 NLT).

Preparations are being made for your arrival. In John 14:2–3 (NKJV) Jesus says: "In My Father's house are many mansions; if it were not so, I would have told you. I go to prepare a place for you. And if I go and prepare a place for you, I will come again and receive you to Myself; that where I am, there you may be also."

Spend time watching home improvement shows, pick a design that resonates with you, spend the cash needed to make it real, and in the end it will never compare favorably to the place being prepared for you when life puts a final exclamation point on your earth story.

If this all seems a little uncomfortable, then you should know that while you're here God guides the steps of each day's plans. In those moments of struggle in your present condition of dust and bones, God compares the *here and now* with the *there and future*. Romans 8:18–21 (MSG) says, "I don't think there's any comparison between the present hard times and the coming good times. The created world itself can hardly wait for what's coming next. Everything in creation is being more or less held back. God reins it in until both creation and all the creatures are ready and can be released at the same moment into the glorious times ahead. Meanwhile, the joyful anticipation deepens."

You could be in a place where the high-gloss shine of life on earth has lost its sparkle. You don't long for death as much as you long for a face-to-face relationship with the God who offered an eternal family gathering with Him in heaven, and you can't think of anything you'd rather do. He may have present plans for you so don't give up, but never let go of that deep joyful anticipation. When that day comes it will be a much better than even trade.

This life is a journey, and you've seen evidence of that excursion in each page of this book. Since it's a journey there must be a destination. If there's a destination there must be a longing to reach the finish line. If there's a finish line there is a place of rest. You'll have stories about the good, bad, and troublesome. Then again, maybe those stories melt away in the heat of God's love. In eternity there may be only one thing you'll be interested in hearing: "Well done, good and faithful servant!" (Matthew 25:21 NIV).

Your time breathing the air of this world is a limited engagement event. James 4:14 (NLT) is a reminder that "your life is like the morning fog—it's here a little while, then it's gone."

Shake yourself free of any feeling that this idea is morbid. God Himself inspired these words: "Precious in the sight of the LORD is the death of His saints" (Psalm 116:15 NKJV). While you might associate death with sorrow, God looks forward to a reunion with you. He knows there is nothing on earth that can compare to what you will experience with Him. In this seemingly odd bit of good news there is hope, there is joy, there is a forever home. Don't race to get there early, but when it's time don't fear the blessed exchange.

He's Prepared to Comfort

Even though I walk through the valley of the shadow of death,
I will fear no evil, for you are with me; your rod and your staff,
they comfort me. You prepare a table before me in the presence
of my enemies; you anoint my head with oil; my cup overflows.
Surely goodness and mercy shall follow me all the days of my
life, and I shall dwell in the house of the LORD forever.
PSALM 23:4–6 ESV

The Great Craftsman

"No eye has seen, no ear has heard, and no mind has
imagined what God has prepared for those who love him."
1 CORINTHIANS 2:9 NLT

Dear God, I have guessed what heaven must be like,
but sometimes I can't get past the clouds, halos, wings,
and harps. You never described heaven those ways, but
others have said it for so long that I have a wrong picture
of my everlasting home. I haven't seen, I haven't heard,
and I can't begin to imagine what the greatest craftsman
of all time has made just for me. Amen.

The Storehouse

"Do not lay up for yourselves treasures on earth, where moth and rust destroy and where thieves break in and steal."
MATTHEW 6:19 NKJV

Dear God, all I can claim ownership of is things—the broken, in-need-of-repair things I will outgrow and throw away. My treasures here can rust, decay, and burn. They can be sold, traded, and stolen. You think so little of my things that You leave them here when I come to see You. Help me remember that my treasure has always been in your storehouse and it waits for me there. May I pay more attention to You than my things. Amen.

Heaven-Bound Quest

"Lay up for yourselves treasures in heaven, where neither moth nor rust destroys and where thieves do not break in and steal."
MATTHEW 6:20 NKJV

Dear God, Your storehouse is safe. Your heaven is secure. Your heart is my home. May I be willing to allow my things to be destroyed if it means I can become closer to You. I know that You are aware of my needs, so help me concentrate on my heavenly home, and sharing You with others so perhaps they will join me in this heaven-bound quest. Amen.

Transformed Desires

"Where your treasure is, there your heart will be also."
MATTHEW 6:21 NKJV

Dear God, if my treasure is a riding mower, then my heart will be in the garage. If my treasure is in a boat, my heart will be on the water. If my treasure is a car, my heart will be in the repair shop. But if my treasure is in You, then my goals change, my desires are transformed, and my choices reflect a heart that rests with You. Amen.

The Reward of the Faithful

Without faith it is impossible to please God, because anyone who comes to him must believe that he exists and that he rewards those who earnestly seek him.
HEBREWS 11:6 NIV

Dear God, my heart trusts what my mind believes. When I walk by faith I begin to see where You lead. When I choose my own way I can't seem to see Your path. You say You reward those who are earnest about seeking You. Help my seeking to be classified as earnest. My future rests in the reward of the faithful. Amen.

My New Address

*We are waiting for new heavens and
a new earth in which righteousness dwells.*
2 PETER 3:13 ESV

Dear God, one of the best things about heaven is that
it's the address for righteousness. The sins associated with
violence, injustice, envy, and gossip will not be allowed.
This is a home where I won't have to pray for my
enemies because God's love makes friends and family
out of strained relationships and hard hearts. I'm
looking forward to my new address. Amen.

The Thief and the Savior

*"A thief is only there to steal and kill and destroy.
I came so they can have real and eternal life,
more and better life than they ever dreamed of."*
JOHN 10:10 MSG

Dear God, I'm here on earth and I have battled an enemy
who wants to take what he did not earn, destroy what was
never his, and kill hopes, dreams, and lives. You have over-
come this common enemy, a thief by trade, and You have
made me an offer—life here and life in the place You've
prepared for me. My imagination lacks the ability to paint
a picture of this glory to come, but I will keep dreaming,
and in the dreaming I will long to see Your face. Amen.

Sidewalk Seams and Berry Plucking

"Look at the birds of the air; they do not sow or reap or store away in barns, and yet your heavenly Father feeds them. Are you not much more valuable than they?"
MATTHEW 6:26 NIV

Dear God, I've seen birds take bits of my food, discover seeds in the seams of sidewalks, and pluck berries from trees. You take care of them, and they don't hesitate to thank You by singing gratitude songs. I watch this as I embrace some internal worry because I face difficulties of my own. Your future for me is not anxiety and stress, but the equivalent of seeds discovered by the birds You take care of. You say I am valuable to You. Help me trust my future to Your ability to provide. Amen.

True Reality

Faith shows the reality of what we hope for; it is the evidence of things we cannot see.
HEBREWS 11:1 NLT

Dear God, some people think Your ideas are foolish because they don't understand them. They don't understand them because they don't believe. When I trust You I get to see more of what You are doing in my life and the world around me. I am not alone, and You are working in this world. My hope has been deposited in Your bank and the investment will be seen in eternity— because I believed before I ever saw. Amen.

One Foot in Front of the Other

We want each of you to show this same diligence to the very end, so that what you hope for may be fully realized.
HEBREWS 6:11 NIV

Dear God, You ask me to be tireless, dedicated, earnest, and diligent. Not just today, but to the very end of life. My faith rests here, right next to the assurance of hope. This is the ultimate in delayed gratification. You have so much waiting for me in the life to come and it is the result of a steady trust, rock-solid hope, and a dedication to put one foot in front of the other on my way to You. Walk with me. I need the encouragement. Amen.

The Business of Today

We expectantly wait for a satisfying relationship with the Spirit. For in Christ, neither our most conscientious religion nor disregard of religion amounts to anything. What matters is something far more interior: faith expressed in love.
GALATIANS 5:5–6 MSG

Dear God, my best efforts don't impress You, and my worst efforts are forgiven. You care about my actions, but You care more about a relationship. You want me to spend my days receiving Your love and passing it on. Those love gifts should never stop and should identify me as one of Your own. This is the business of today and the plan for tomorrow. And in eternity it will be the breath of my existence. Amen.

Conclusion

The Power of Bold Steps

God created dads to leave a legacy. He created dads to invest in the lives of their families. He created dads to be men after His own heart. He wants you to step up and allow Him to help you fill shoes He made for you to wear.

By the time you reach the bottom of this page the thoughts expressed in this book will conclude, but there is more God can teach you. Twenty-one aspects of a dad's life have been expressed here. Nearly two hundred brief prayers have been written to lead you to a conversation with God. Don't stop praying or reading! Explore God's Word on additional subjects that interest you. Take some of the verses and craft them into personalized prayers.

In many cases once the last word in any book has been read, there is a sense of satisfaction in having finished the book. This is followed by a warm feeling that you learned something. You may have gravitated to a few thoughts that had meaning for you in this book. What will you do with it?

Maybe something in this book can move beyond recreational reading. You are encouraged to take even one topic addressed here and put it to work in your everyday life. You may want to share a few thoughts with others, including the God who made and loves you.

This book began in prayer, includes prayer, and encourages prayer throughout its pages. Don't stop praying. Instead, continue your God conversation.

Scripture Index